Early Vermont Broadsides

The University Press of New England

SPONSORING INSTITUTIONS

Brandeis University
Clark University
Dartmouth College
The University of New Hampshire
The University of Rhode Island
The University of Vermont

Early Vermont Broadsides

John Duffy, Editor

Introduction by Mason I. Lowance, Jr.

Published for the University of Vermont by the *University Press of New England* Hanover New Hampshire 1975

Library of Congress Catalogue Card Number 74-12541
International Standard Book Number 0-87451-108-9
Printed in the United States of America

Contents

Acknowledgments

We are particulary indebted to Georgia Bumgardner, the Andrew Mellon Curator of Graphic Arts at the American Antiquarian Society, for valuable suggestions and for the use of research materials from her book *American Broadsides*. The staffs of the Vermont Historical Society, the American Antiquarian Society, and the Huntington Library and Art Gallery have also been most helpful.

Two books of great importance for students of the culture of both Vermont and the Republic during the late eighteenth and early nineteenth centuries were used extensively. The debt owed Ola Elizabeth Winslow, whose early work on American broadside verse has been widely known since it was first published in 1930, is evident from the number of times her book is cited below. And this collection would not have been attempted, let alone completed, without the invaluable compilation of information in Marcus McCorison's *Vermont Imprints, 1778–1820*.

For permission to publish broadsides from their collections, we are grateful to the John Carter Brown Library of Brown University, the Dartmouth College Library, the Library Company of Philadelphia, the Shelburne Museum, the American Antiquarian Society, and the Vermont Historical Society.

For their support of the publication of this collection we wish to thank Dean William H. Macmillan of the Graduate College, University of Vermont, and William G. Craig, Chancellor of the Vermont State Colleges.

December 1974 J.D.
M.I.L.

Introduction

On April 13, 1973, the United States Post Office issued a stamp commemorating the "Rise of the Spirit of Independence." The engraving depicts an energetic and determined man nailing a revolutionary broadside to a wooden door while a crowd of colonial citizens gathers to read it. The implication of the scene portrayed is that a correspondence exists between the public declaration of principle on broadsides and the growing sentiment for independence. Appropriately, the stamp is part of the observance of the Bicentennial of the American Revolution.

The stamp designers were correct in associating strong public feeling with the distribution of broadsides, and they were particularly astute in suggesting that broadsides of the revolutionary era which were displayed in prominent public places stimulated the growth and dissemination of ideas. One critical use of broadsides, from the time they first appeared in the fifteenth century to the present day, has been as a vehicle for public pronouncement, whether by officials of the government or by individuals. It is significant that the first examples of printing both in Europe and in New England were broadsides rather than books. The earliest dated specimen of printing from movable type was a broadside "Letter of Indulgence" granted by Pope Nicholas V, in aid of John II against the Turks, April 12, 1451, shortly after the invention of printing in 1450.[1] Martin Luther exploited the common custom of posting a broadside when he nailed his famous Ninety-Five Theses to the door of the church in Wittenburg in 1519, although he had not printed his lengthy declaration against Rome. And in the Anglo-American colonies, Stephen Daye's little press in Cambridge issued "The Freeman's Oath" in 1639, one year prior to the printing of the famous *Bay Psalm Book* (1640).[2] Following these early examples of religious and political proclamation, the broadside has served as a primary vehicle for the dissemination of news and the broadcasting of information in a myriad of causes. Even today the broadside and its relatives, the newspaper and periodical, have not been superseded by other media as a means of inspiring public reaction, and the printed word is still a source of final authority for many people. The broadside is particularly suitable for editorializing, moralizing, and offering commentary on events as they occur. Moreover, it is possible to trace the development of opinion by comparing one printed argument with the responses it generates in support or in opposition. Thus when the colonists finally declared their independence from Great Britain on July 4, 1776, the original manuscript document was quickly printed as a broadside that was circulated throughout the colonies and in England. It was, with the newspaper versions, the most effective and dramatic way to justify the revolution publicly. Broadsides have not always been recognized as historical literature, but they are certainly important to our understanding of the historical events many of them announce. As fragmentary chronicles of public events, they often are more dramatic than newspaper accounts of familiar episodes, because of the urgency with which

1. Ola E. Winslow, *American Broadside Verse from Imprints of the 17th and 18th Centuries* (New Haven, 1930), p. xvii.

2. The first American printing had been done one hundred years earlier by Juan Pablos in Mexico, who operated a press for Juan Cromberger, one of the leading printers of Seville. See the Catholic primer by Juan de Zumarraga, Archbishop of Mexico, printed in 1544, just one of many early imprints from the Pablos press.

they are usually issued and the eye-catching format in which they are sometimes printed.

A broadside is a single sheet of paper printed on one side only. When printed on both sides, the publication is usually termed a broadsheet, and when folded and printed on four sides, a periodical, a pamphlet, or a newspaper.[3] But these narrow definitions suggest little of the broadside's role as a cultural artifact. Moreover, the variety of broadsides makes them difficult to classify or define as a group. Nor is the verse that has appeared on them very distinguished. Ola Elizabeth Winslow, an authority on American broadsides, has noted that "broadside verse is, of course, not a literary *genre*. The broadside was merely a medium of circulation, restricted to timely subjects of an urgent nature. Poetry of another sort might be quietly passed to one's friend in manuscript copies or await dignified publication in book form. Not so the message of the hour. It must be printed at once and was doubtless forgotten as quickly." [4] Though this judgment may appear to be harsh, it is accurate when broadside verse is judged as literature. Even the broadside poems of well-known early American writers like Royall Tyler are not representative of their best talents. Unfortunately, it is the failure of the broadside to fit conveniently into a literary classification that has contributed to its neglect.

If the verse that frequently appeared on broadsides cannot be considered a literary genre, the broadside itself can be discussed as a literary type, with a history and function not unlike that of the newspaper or periodical essay. Though not all of the information carried on broadsides was urgent, the Revolutionary broadside, for example, was usually associated with a particular event or occasion. The broadside has eluded the literary historian partly because the conventions of broadside authorship do not conveniently follow the patterns of literary attribution. There are few well-recognized "broadside authors"; in fact, most broadsides cannot be attributed to a single writer. Many are not signed at all, thus allowing just about anyone to assert practically anything at all without having to take responsibility. On the other hand, when broadsides appeared at the time of the resistance to British domination of the colonies, printers guilty of publishing revolutionary documents attacking the British not only were legally endangered, but their lives and property were jeopardized. Isaiah Thomas, the New England printer who founded the American Antiquarian Society, to escape the British, moved his press from Boston to Worcester, where it still remains as part of the Society's collection. But the broadside has traditionally offered the political world a spectrum of expression ranging from the most polite and commendatory proclamation to the most inflammatory political invective. In all cases the declarations are intended to generate a public response, and a good example of how the early broadside did the work of modern underground newspapers is seen in one that appeared at the time of the Tea Act in 1774:

BRETHREN AND FELLOW CITIZENS

You may depend that those odious Miscreants and detestable Tools to the Ministry and Governor, the Tea Consignees (those traitors to their country, Butchers, who have done, and are doing everything to Murder and Destroy all that shall stand in the way of the private Interest) are determined to come and reside again in the Town of Boston. I therefore give you this early Notice, that you may hold yourselves in Readiness, on the shortest Notice, to give them such a Reception as such vile ingrates deserve.

Joyce, Jun.
Chairman of the Committee
of Tarring and Feathering [5]

3. Georgia Bumgardner, *American Broadsides* (Barre, Massachusetts, 1971), introduction.

4. Winslow, *American Broadside Verse*, p. xix.

5. See Samuel Tower, "Broadsides for the Revolution," *New York Times* (Sunday, March 25, 1973), where the text of this broadside is printed.

It is the public nature of the broadside that gives it a unique place in documentary history and makes special demands on students of literature. Though nearly all broadsides were designed to make a statement about a particular situation or occasion, a large number of them survive today, a surprising fact if one considers the scarcity of paper in colonial times and realizes that the blank side of a broadside made an ideal surface for other kinds of writing. It seems clear that the amateur archivists of the early period realized the value of the broadside for preserving important moments of cultural history. Initially, they are critical to our understanding of the events to which they immediately relate. For example, Paul Revere's masterful engraving of the Boston Massacre and the narrative that accompanied it became a well-known description of the events of that tragic day in 1770. Ultimately, the Revere engraving and the story became more than a simple documentary account of recent events. Brief and one-sided, the narrative and its picture became a symbol of British tyranny, and the publication of the document an act of highest patriotism.

Thus broadsides must be considered in the cultural context out of which they arise and to which they so graphically contribute. It is this principle of cultural interaction that should govern our reading of broadsides, although the traditional method of classifying them still provides a very useful means of grouping the various topics contained in them. The highly inflammatory Revere broadside is a political document entitled "The Bloody Massacre perpetrated in King-Street, Boston, on March 5, 1770, by a party of the 29th Regt." But further investigation of its provenance indicates that it may not have been intended simply as a broadside. As Hitchings points out, "many copies from the original printing survive; many of them are in their original frames with the original glass still in place. Revere apparently sold them framed and glazed. You could issue a broadside framed, of course, but the value obviously placed upon the *Boston Massacre* seems to identify it first as a picture, after all, and one meant to last. Not all broadsides were throwaways, but almost by definition, they are printed for the moment." [6]

The importance Revere attached to the massacre broadside indicates the kind of response he anticipated, and it provides an example of the broadside's important relation to an audience for which it was specifically designed. It is this moment of interaction that we must catch in reviewing broadsides as historical documents of cultural significance. It is impossible to understand them properly if they are approached with no concern for the circumstances which produced them. But viewed in the historical context, the broadside can become a window to much larger and more wide-ranging events, and in some cases, can provide insight into the attitudes and values of a local group.

The varied uses of the broadsides are too numerous even to catalog accurately. State governors issue broadsides to proclaim special days or recognize an individual for meritorious service. Large circus posters (those published by Barnum and Bailey, for example) are available today, and on university campuses in America and Europe the broadside is one of the most common forms of advertising forthcoming events. Modern direct-mail advertising also employs broadsides to circulate information, and while the sociological function of the document has altered, the form has remained essentially the same. Because the broadside cannot really exist outside a particular cultural context, however, it is necessary to group the documents within a historical framework according to topics that were prominent at the time.

The time-frame for understanding the broadsides represented in the present collection is that of revolutionary and postrevolutionary New England. The earliest document in the collection is "To the Inhabitants of

6. Sinclair Hitchings, "A Broadside View of America," *Lithopinion*, Vol. 5, Issue 17, Number 1 (Spring 1970), p. 69.

Vermont, a Free and Independent State, bounding on the River Connecticut and Lake Champlain," and it was printed in April of 1777. The latest copy is of "A Wonderful Dream, by Dr. Isaac Watts, author of Psalms and Hymns," and it was made in 1821. During this period, the state of Massachusetts dominated New England broadside production, primarily because Massachusetts had a running head start on other colonies in establishing printing as an industry. Indeed, many Vermont notices were printed in Massachusetts prior to the first establishment of a Vermont press in 1779.[7]

Although the earliest American broadside was an official political document (The Freeman's Oath), and although the political broadside has dominated the production in New England, broadsides bearing funeral elegies were the first type to appear. Later histories of early New England, such as Nathaniel Morton's *New Englands Memoriall* (1669) and Cotton Mather's *Magnalia Christi Americana* (1702) contain examples of broadside elegies for which the original documents no longer survive. Morton's history records broadside verses for Peter Bulkley and John Cotton, who were mourned by Thomas Hooker, and similar lamentations for John Cotton penned by Benjamin Wood and John Norton. Although these verses are considered to be the earliest American broadsides on record, the earliest *surviving* American broadside elegiac imprint was made by Perciful Lowle for John Winthrop, who died in 1649.[8]

The funeral elegy and elegiac broadside had a specific sociological function. The verse was usually crude and ill-constructed, since it was most likely written with great haste at the time of death. Broadside elegies often were, however, the only public expression of grief over the departed. Samuel Sewall's *Diary* alludes to such a custom in America. After attending the funeral of the Rev. Thomas Shepard, June 9, 1685, Sewall wrote, "It seems there were some Verses; but non pinned on the Herse." Ola Winslow points out that "since early colonial burials were conducted with rigid simplicity as to ritual, it is probable that no ceremony attended the presentation of these memorials. They merely provided a silent outlet for the expression of grief, and an opportunity to honor the dead. Often one person was thus honored by numerous tributes." [9]

Two funeral elegies appear in this collection, "Lines written by Lucy Winn on the Death of Abner Wright, June 3, 1812," and "A Poem, composed on the Death of Mr. Stephen Batcheller, and Mr. Denison Gallup, who were both drowned at Queechy Falls, in Connecticut River, on the 5th of August, 1805." In form and stanzaic structure, the two elegies are similar, and they also agree on the general subject treated: death. In the response each generated with a particular readership, however, they are quite different.

The Lucy Winn elegy for Abner Wright is the more conventional of the two. It begins with an admonition to the "dying sons of men" and narrates in straightforward, simple manner the facts about Abner Wright's life and death. We learn that he was forty-one years old and that he died of consumption. We are also told that he left a widow and sister. But most of the twenty quatrains are devoted to moralizing, and the deceased becomes a specter in the imagination of the author and reader:

Come sinners now forewarned be,
Religion's a reallity,
Remember tho' he's out of sight,
You soon must meet with Abner Wright.

The thrust of the elegy is that of warning and admonition; the survivors and readers are

7. See Elizabeth F. Cooley, *Vermont Imprints before 1800: An Introductory Essay on the History of Printing in Vermont, 1779–1799* (Montpelier, Vermont, 1937), and Marcus McCorison, *Vermont Imprints, 1778–1820* (Worcester, Massachusetts, 1963). The exhaustive McCorison bibliography supersedes the Cooley study.

8. Winslow, p. xix.

9. Ibid.

cautioned against allowing too much time to elapse before making arrangements for death. The final quatrain echoes Psalm 103:

All flesh like grass does quickly fade,
And man beneath the ground is laid,
O may we then prepared be
To reign with Christ eternally.

The second broadside also presents two elegiac tragedies, the result of accidental drownings. Stephen Batcheller and Denison Gallup were drowned in the Connecticut River on August 5, 1805. The narrative account makes little of the fact that "Young GALLUP, his friend for to save, / Rush'd into the dangers around; / There sunk in the watery grave . . ." Both youths are grouped together in a tragic narrative that is conventional and formulaic. The classical elements are present: angels and seraph sing, and the departed are mourned by parents, relatives, and friends. But the tragedy is attended by a triumphant note. In the first of two poems in the broadside we find the following assurance:

Soon, Gabriel's *loud trumpet shall sound*
And bid my fair STEPHEN *arise,*
No longer to sleep in the ground,
But rise to his God in the skies.

In the second poem, addressed specifically to Denison Gallup, a similar triumph is prophesied:

Sleep then, sweet youth, till that bright morn,
When Christ your body shall adorn,
With his own likeness clear and bright,
Then mount to worlds of purest light.

Obviously, these elegies are not the sophisticated neoclassical elegiac poetry that preceded their publication during the Renaissance and Augustan periods in England, nor do they measure favorably when compared to the funeral elegies written by New England Puritans of the seventeenth century, many of which were both classical and Christian in treatment, rivaling the best-regarded work of the English renaissance. These Vermont elegies, rather, should be considered as a special kind of New England art, primitive and unusual, like the wall paintings of the period. The lack of sophistication and the simple approach to the mournful circumstances are manifestations of the cultural conditions out of which the verses arose. In the cases of Batcheller and Gallup, the broadside elegies are doubtless the only public notice given their passing and, as such, would be both obituary and funeral eulogy for the two departed boys.

Grouped with these elegiac verses are two verse-songs and another poem. The "Bold Lads of Canada" deserves special attention because it presents the British point of view on the conflict with "Yankee Boys," and concludes "Here's a health to all the British troops," while "A Christmas Hymn," by Royall Tyler, the well-known revolutionary-era dramatist and poet from Vermont, is a conventional Christmas devotion composed to be sung. It follows the Psalm tune structure for tune-books of the time for Psalm 148.[10]

The "Wonderful Dream" of Isaac Watts is a narrative poem depicting a vision of the Judgment and a deliverance from Satan's grasp that is suitable to climax these elegiac verses that also emphasize the imminence of the last days.

The poem opens in the late evening, "When the bright monarch of the day / Withdrew from human sight," and almost immediately the reader is thrust into a mysterious vision, in which an angel appears to the narrator. "Swiftly he bore me by the hand, / Through the etherial blue, / Leaving the lesser orbs of light, / And higher planets too." In the tradition of Dante's *Divine Comedy* and other medieval visions of the afterlife, the poem is designed to be a visionary journey into worlds other than our own, "Thro' liquid realms and starry plains." The dreamer sees almost at

10. See John Tufts, *Introduction to the Singing of Psalm Tunes*, 5th ed. (Boston, 1726); and Josiah Flagg, *Collection of the Best Psalm Tunes* (Boston, 1764).

once a view of the Garden of Eden and the "shining spires" of Jerusalem, which are the standard stuff of medieval dream visions, which, in turn, were based on the prophetic descriptions contained in the Book of Revelation. But in this vision the dreamer perceives a "monstrous shape," which he immediately understands to be the "black infernal prince," the "proudest of rebels." Like his medieval counterparts, the dreamer participates in the action he narrates, and enters into a dialogue with the Devil, with whom he argues about his own salvation. Reminiscent of Michael Wigglesworth's dramatic poem "The Day of Doom" (1662), which also depicts the judgment, the Devil declares:

For sins surprising red,
Before the awful bar of GOD,
You'll presently be had.
Where, from the glorious Judge's mouth,
Thy sentence will proceed . . . .

But the dreamer answers this challenge with the faith of a true believer:

'Tis true I have provok'd my GOD,
But JESUS CHRIST has dy'd
To save the humble simple soul
From hell's incessant pains,
And he will keep my soul secure
From your infernal chains.

This confidence in Christ's deliverance of repentant sinners is justified. Soon after the dialogue with Satan, the dreamer sees

. . . a lofty, shining throne . . .
On adamantine pillars rais'd,
Most glorious to behold.
On this the blessed JESUS sat,
The Father's *chief delight,*
Cloath'd with a long unspotted robe,
Like snow unsullied white.

The resplendent trope is momentarily transformed as Jesus takes out the "numerous leaves" which contain "the fates of mortal men." The apprehension of the dreamer about his own fate is shared by the reader, who is given a graphic description of the slow motion process by which the individual fate is learned from the "Book." But at last, the dreamer is told by Jesus: "in this list of blessed souls / I also set thy name," and the poet's attitude shifts from apprehension to joy.

But the drama has not ended. The Devil, after all, has only receded momentarily. He reappears, after this Judgment scene, to say: "Your hope of grace is vain / For I will surely win your soul, / By tempting you again." Watts has brought together the medieval dream vision and the Faust-motif, and the poem concludes dramatically with a dismissal of the Devil from the dreamer's presence. After a long section describing the history of Satan's work in God's earthly paradise, the dreamer assures the devil (and the reader) that grace is irresistible and that he will continue to be a saint regardless of Satan's efforts to tempt him. The dreamer and his angelic guide last see the fiend clawing the ground in a bestial rage engendered by his failure to win the dreamer's soul. The poem ends with the dreamer awakening from his vision, which brings the narrative full circle. Of the poems contained in this volume, this one is clearly the most literary, employing conventions and tropes that were common literary devices at the time of the poem's composition.

The second group of broadsides of the present book, "Inventions, Discoveries, and Public Announcements," represents what probably was the most intriguing type of broadside produced during the colonial period and nineteenth century in America. The curious feature of the advertisement for "Hubbel's New Invented Water Wheel" is its proclamation of a patent claim. Patents were few in the postrevolutionary period, considering New England's claim for Yankee ingenuity, but Vermont had more than a proportional share. The main paragraph of the broadside gives the modern reader an interesting picture of a particular agricultural problem and indicates that even in 1806 farming and science were developing together. Though the farmer would have been dependent on the mill owner for the grinding of his corn into meal, he would have been familiar with the mechanical advantages of the Hubbel water wheel.

A less specialized announcement is the broadside declaring a "Reparation Lottery," which clearly associates patriotism and the support of state government with the purchase of one of the three thousand tickets. The spirit of this lottery has survived today. State governments treat practitioners of the "numbers game" as criminal violators of the law; lotteries operated by the state are common, however, particularly in the Northeast, where earlier the Puritans imposed harsh sentences on anyone caught gambling for profit. New York, New Hampshire, and Massachusetts now have well-established lottery systems, which provide revenue for a variety of government services.

By far the most well-preserved and numerous broadsides in collections like that of the Vermont Historical Society and the American Antiquarian Society are those containing political announcements. There are two reasons. First, the government rarely charged for their announcements. Other broadsides, particularly those containing verses of a commemorative nature, were sold in the streets by hawkers. Government proclamations, on the contrary, were usually posted in prominent places. Because they were produced at public expense, they were generally printed in greater quantity, and that is a second reason why more copies of these political broadsides survive. Among the collection of the Vermont Historical Society, almost all of the broadsides for which there is more than one copy are political.

The political or governmental broadside can be a fascinating document. In the present collection both the "Military Announcements" and those treating "Politics and Statecraft" are in this category. Consider the excitement generated among the eyewitnesses to the naval engagement on Lake Champlain on September 11, 1814, when the American naval forces under Captain Thomas Macdonough defeated the British fleet, while British armies were also being repulsed at Plattsburgh. The paintings and engravings depicting this colorful engagement provide a visual complement to the two broadsides included here, which also depict the conflicts. In the *Northern Sentinel* "Extra" for September 13, 1814, Macdonough is declared the hero of the day. Here, he is seen as a strictly military figure, and the statistical approach to the victory taken by the *Sentinel* editor seems to anticipate the detailed reporting that allows modern readers to objectify the newspaper accounts of battles and military conflicts. The ever-present "body count" is a traditional measurement of the success of the winning side, with little thought to the principles involved for either group. The concluding line, set in italic, echoes the confidence in Divine Providence shared by the Vermont settlers of another generation: *To the interposition of heaven, be ascribed our glorious victory.*

The most impressive document of this group is the large broadside entitled "The Battle of P[l]attsburgh." It is more than the celebration of a single victory. Four "songs" appear on it, running in columns down the page. First, "A Yankee Song," called "The Retreat of the English from New-Orleans," celebrates that disastrous battle with rhetorical flourish:

> *Such carnage ne'er was known before;*
> *More than three thousand stain our shore,*
> *And some assert a thousand more*
> *Of the proud foes of Orleans. . . .*
>
> *A bloodless victory, on our side,*
> *May well increase our general's pride;*
> *For see——the field is only dyed*
> *With* English *blood near Orleans.*

The emblem at the top of the column venerates Andrew Jackson as "The Second WASHINGTON of America," and despite the inconclusive combat of New Orleans, Jackson is elevated to the stature of conquerer and hero:

Here's to the gallant General *who!*
Has saved our town and country too!
A braver man the world ne'er knew,
Than he who fought for Orleans.

The second song and central verse describes the Battle of Plattsburgh in eight-line stanzas with a rollicking beat and doggerel verse form. Some of the rhyme makes the conflict seem almost comic, but the message is clear: the British were routed. The third song, celebrating "Commodore Macdonough's Victory," is composed in quatrains, or four-line stanzas. There is more of a martial quality to this song, and one of the most unusual lines is that containing the word "Columbia" as a reference to America or the United States, a new term first coined by Timothy Dwight in his 1777 song by that name. The term was in common use by 1816, the actual date of the printing, though the date it carries is 1815, an error corrected in later printings. The final song of the broadside is its finest, the "Battle of Niagara! or, America again victorious over her white and red savage Enemies!" The verse is ballad meter; the rhythm is haunting and the narrative effective. One can imagine reading or chanting this verse to children in an attempt to build up a mythlike history of contemporary American events. The final stanza is followed by a woodcut that is clearly out of place: it depicts a woman holding an umbrella under a palm tree, with an island and trees in the background, complete with pagoda. The cut was no doubt originally designed for a book about travels in oriental lands, and the woman is clearly oriental in dress and character, but the caption for the emblem is "COLUMBIA, finally victorious over all her enemies—reclining in Peace, and surrounded with plenty." Although this may echo the pastoral and millennial theme so common in the celebration of the virtues of the New Republic, it is hardly commensurate with the woodcut with which it is associated. Visually, however, the broadside is superb, containing some thirty-three separate cuts, including one of Neptune with his trident as a representation of the British "Capt. Downie," who died on his ship at Plattsburgh. Despite these inaccuracies of fact and composition, it remains one of the most elegant examples of early Vermont broadside printing.

"A Review of New England Politics" is a broadside containing "two letters from a Clergyman," who was Ignatius Thomson, the Jeffersonian patriot who edited two New England school books in addition to his duties as minister to the Pomfret Congregational Church. These letters are not anonymous eyewitness accounts to large public events but are the equivalent of a modern, signed editorial. Thomson is urged on by a pressing need: "The design of the Congressional [sic] clergy have become so alarming to the freedom of religious enquiry, and the liberties of our country, (for they are intimately connected), I cannot feel excused any longer to remain in silence." The issues about which he feels compelled to speak include the misunderstandings generated among his fellow clergymen about his political stands, and the second letter is particularly addressed to the problem of Calvinism in the control of New England colleges. As a broadside, this document illustrates the use of the medium for the dissemination of personal views, a practice that often gave men in public life the opportunity to state their cases on given issues that had become confused or misunderstood in the absence of instant communications and the predominance of gossip and rumor spreading. Of course, there was no provision for "equal time," but the presses were always active with the publication of "rejoinders," so that sometimes an argument between two hostile factions would appear in a series of broadsides that extended over a period of time.

All of the broadsides in the last two groups in this collection have some connection with local political problems, including the dreams and visions that are allegorical treatments of current events.

One document deserves special mention, however, not for its uniqueness, but for its conventional format and "representative" qualities. "By His Excellency Thomas Chittenden," October 18, 1778, is a conventional announcement by which the Governor would declare a day of thanksgiving, in this case the celebration of a traditional Thanksgiving Day. These thanksgiving proclamations contain a large amount of political rhetoric, but they have a way of revealing values and attitudes which more private documents or more specifically occasional broadsides cannot achieve. Though the newly formed republic stood firmly on a separation of the powers of church and state—unlike its Puritan and colonial predecessors, who lived in Massachusetts Bay Colony in a theocracy that was equally committed to the union of church and state—the thanksgiving broadside does more than ask the blessing of God on a humble venture: it specifically echoes theological ideas that were prominent among the Puritans and persist into modern times. Thanks is given for the usual "divine Interposition in raising up a powerful Ally in Favor of the United States," a clear allusion to France's role in the revolutionary cause; but the broadside also expresses the wish that "God would yet make us glad, according to the Days wherein we have been afflicted, and the Time in which we have seen Evil . . . That this once howling Wilderness may, in a spiritual sense, bud and blossom like the Rose:—That he will be pleased to bless and prosper the Work of our Hands;—Establish his Covenant with us and our Children to the latest Posterity:—And fill the Universe with a Display of his glorious Perfections, through our Lord and Saviour, Jesus Christ." These specific echoes of the Puritan errand into the wilderness and the covenant theology on which that doctrine was based indicate that the revolutionary mind was still occupied with the idea of governance within the framework of Divine Providence, by which all things would be ultimately accomplished. Whether or not the Rationalists like Jefferson and Franklin who framed the Constitution believed what they wrote, they delivered their enlightenment beliefs in the rhetoric of conventional and traditional theology, indicating how strongly public attitudes were still governed by the views of the early settlers of New England. It is interesting that Thanksgiving broadsides to this day contain apostrophes to God's eternal Providence.

The social significance of such a conventional document goes beyond the immediate circumstances that occasion its publication. In a number of thanksgiving proclamations of the early nineteenth century, for example, appeals were made to the citizenry to "learn to Christianize the Indians, and not to exterminate them," as was stated in a Caleb Strong broadside for 1812.

Political broadsides, however, will continue to fascinate primarily for the specific events they illuminate. As Shipton put it: "The Massachusetts Puritans were alone among their contemporaries in thinking that the people should be informed of all legislation, and provide for it by law, setting up the Cambridge Press in defiance of Parliamentary statute as serious as a defiance in the coining of pine tree shillings. In Bay Colony days the members of the legislature carried home at the end of each session broadside printings of the laws to be exhibited at town meeting." [11] Massachusetts may have been ahead of her neighbor states in making all constitutional transactions available immediately, but she was hardly alone, as the broadsides in this volume attest—for example, "To the People of Vermont," or "In Congress, May 15, 1776 . . . To the Inhabitants of Vermont, A Free and Independent State, bounding on the River Connecticut and Lake Champlain," or "State of Vermont. In Council, Windsor, 7th June, 1779." These documents specify legal and constitutional details that would often be overlooked even in some newspaper accounts of the time. And as examples of the work of a free press, they are superb contributions to the social history of the United States.

Of the four broadsides in the last group, "Dreams, Visions, Providences, and Narrative

11. Clifford Shipton, *Some Early Massachusetts Broadsides* (Boston, 1964), foreword.

Poems," only the first, the vision of Samuel Ingalls, lacks an illustration. All four of these documents, however, have profoundly significant political implications, as explained in the editor's note for each. Often the British were depicted as being tyrannical, but in these broadsides their description as "monstrous" and the employment of earlier graphic conventions to describe a contemporary phenomenon exemplifies the ingenuity that frequently attended broadside production. The Grecian Daughter story, for example, has a very long history, appearing in Pliny's *Naturalis historia* and in the *De factis dictisque memorabilibus* of Valerius Maximus. In the late Middle Ages a version appeared in Boccacio's *De claris mulieribus*, and the story was popular throughout the Renaissance, from which, no doubt, the broadside author's source was taken.

Like other contemporary broadsides, these Vermont documents have a flavor of the time, partly transmitted by the illustrative woodcuts or engravings that accompany the text, as the "Battle of Plattsburgh" clearly illustrates. It is important to realize that these illustrations were not always made specifically for the broadsides in which they appear. As Georgia Bumgardner puts it, "printers had a number of illustrative 'stock' cuts on hand which they gradually accumulated—coffins, skulls and crossed bones, Death with his scythe—which were reused many times without much regard for the text. This was due to simple economics and to the difficulty in finding an artist who could execute the design. The salability of broadsides depended on the speed with which they appeared. A printer just could not wait to issue a ballad about a contemporary event." [12] Woodcut illustrations were perhaps used longer in the making of broadsides than in the decoration of printed books, because they were cheaper and more available after copper and steel engraving became a popular medium. "The use of woodcuts declined after 1800, probably because many of the better printers turned to the technically better illustrations engraved on end-grain wood, or to talented artists who engraved on copper and made aquatints. The woodcut-illustrated broadside, declining in importance, was more likely to be produced by a printer poor in means or provincial in location or attitude." [13] Frequently, in the eighteenth century, cuts were used interchangeably in books and broadsides.

This was not the case with "The Hypocrite's Looking-Glass," published by Isaac Eddy of Weathersfield, Vermont, in 1815. This superb engraving is signed by Eddy, who was well-known for his illustrations of this type, and the example here shows intricate detail and balanced visual perspective. In contrast, the illustrations for "A Monster. Frightful as Ten Furies!! Terrible as Hell!" printed at Windsor, Vermont, in 1812, and "The Grecian Daughter," also printed at Windsor, in 1810, appear to be woodcuts that were not specifically designed for the broadsides in which they appear. Indeed, the allegorical and political interpretations of these legends provided by the editor in the notes to each of these documents would indicate that conventional and traditional formulae were given new meaning by filling the old casks with new wine. Similarly, the coffin illustration for the *Monitor's* "To the People of Vermont" must have come from a stock pool of illustrative materials. It is curious that an illustration would sometimes conflict with information contained in the narrative portions of a broadside, as when a document commemorating a public execution has three bodies dangling from ropes in the illustration and only one or two mentioned in the text.

This introduction would be incomplete without a discussion of the early history of Vermont printing. It is a curious tale, and explains the relatively late development of the industry within the boundaries of the state. Massachusetts and Connecticut clearly held

12. Bumgardner, introduction.

13. Ibid.

the lead in New England printing during the eighteenth century, and it is because of the large-scale availability of printers in these neighboring states that Vermont had no pressing need to develop an industry on her own until the period of the American Revolution. Although many of the broadsides in the present collection were printed in Vermont, the industry was very young at the time they were published, and its practitioners were former apprentices or associates of Massachusetts and Connecticut printers with more established reputations.

John Spargo, the former Director-Curator of the Bennington Historical Museum and Art Gallery, has carefully traced the development of the Vermont printing industry.[14] Spargo notes that when the state of Vermont was formed in 1777, it had not a single printer, but as with the Massachusetts Bay Colony, the formation of the new state necessitated the development of printing, since government documents, broadsides, charters, bills of lading, and other official proclamations needed to be issued regularly by an authorized printer. Judah Paddock Spooner and Alden Spooner, two brothers, had, however, set up a printing house in Dresden (now Hanover, New Hampshire), and in 1778 Eleazar Wheelock, then President of Dartmouth College, persuaded them that the house was important to the state. The Spooners remained in Dresden and were considered the first Vermont printers, although Dresden was one of sixteen towns that were contested by New Hampshire and Vermont in a border dispute resulting from an action by the Vermont legislature on June 11, 1778, to incorporate the sixteen into the State of Vermont. The first imprints by the Spooner press included such famous titles as Ethan Allen's *Vindication of the Opposition of the Inhabitants of Vermont to the Government of New York* and the *Acts and Laws of the State of Vermont in America*.[15]

Toward the end of 1780, Judah Paddock Spooner and Timothy Green established a press at Westminster, Vermont. This was the result of legislative pressure, and Spargo notes that "On October 27th, 1779, [the legislature] set forth that 'it is absolutely necessary that a printing office be erected within the limits of this State, to print the laws that are or may be enacted by the legislature from time to time; to publish a Newspaper under the Signature of the State; and to do other incidental business'." [16] Spooner and Green were the offspring of more famous printers of the same name, but they managed to set up a press that produced broadsides, the Acts and Laws of the State, some paper currency, and a newspaper. Meanwhile, Alden Spooner continued to reside at Hanover.

Another Vermont printer of the period was Anthony Haswell, who came from Springfield, Massachusetts, and who had served an apprenticeship to Isaiah Thomas. In 1783 Haswell settled at Bennington, apparently induced by the promise that he would receive "the patronage of the State." Alden Spooner, who was now in Windsor, also assumed that he was to enjoy the patronage of the state business, and a considerable rivalry between the two printers flourished during the 1780's and 1790's.

> *There was still rivalry between Anthony Haswell and Alden Spooner. The state printing continued to be the subject of vexation and dissatisfaction. In October, 1790, the General Assembly enacted a law providing that "the several laws and other business of the State, shall be printed by Messrs. Haswell and Russell of Bennington on the West Side and Mr. Spooner on the east side of the mountain, alternately as the General Assembly shall be holden on the different sides of the mountain. Provided, They will do the same on as reasonable terms as can be procured from other printers."* [17]

Toward the end of the decade printing became a flourishing industry in the state, and

14. "Early Vermont Printers and Printing," *Vermont History* (December 1942), 214–229.

15. Ibid., p. 218.

16. Ibid., p. 219.

17. Ibid., pp. 223, 226.

individuals like Matthew Lyon, James Hill, Benjamin Smead, Cornelius Sturtevant, George and Robert Waite, and the Rev. Samuel Williams became associated with the politics of the Revolution and with the titles that were issued from their presses. New methods of composition were being developed, and Vermont, like the other states of New England, was moving toward an industrialized society. The following century would see the expansion of printing, and the formation of laws and regulations to govern such struggles as that of Spooner and Haswell. As John Spargo put it:

> *As the eighteenth century ended, Vermont was quite well supplied with local printing offices and newspapers. The day of the old printer-editor, who frequently set up his articles as he mentally composed them, without troubling to write them first, was passing with the century. The new century was to see a rapid specialization of function, printers ceasing to be editors and editorial ranks recruited from outside the printing craft. Such figures as Alden Spooner, Benjamin Smead, Anthony Haswell and James Lyon can only be understood and appreciated when viewed against the background of the social conditions of their time. Long before they passed away, the four pioneer Vermont printers of the eighteenth century had come to be regarded as quaint survivals of a past age.*[18]

The broadsides in the present collection all appeared during this nativity of printing in Vermont. Several of the more striking ones were produced after 1800, but the whole range and flavor of the period is represented in those chosen for the collection. The curious mixture of verse, visual effect, and politics in the "Battle of Plattsburgh," shows how much of the design of the early documents was left to the printer, who might, as he set type, throw into the frame an appropriate woodcut (or an inappropriate one, if it fit the space!). That these early journeymen were able to produce works of quality in spite of the fact that they often labored singlehandedly to produce them is testimony to their high standards.

Vermont is by no means unique in this account, but her story is typical of New England as a region, where one of the first acts of the new settlers was the establishing of a university at Cambridge, followed soon by the creation of an American press.

18. Ibid., p. 229.

Verses, Psalms, & Hymns

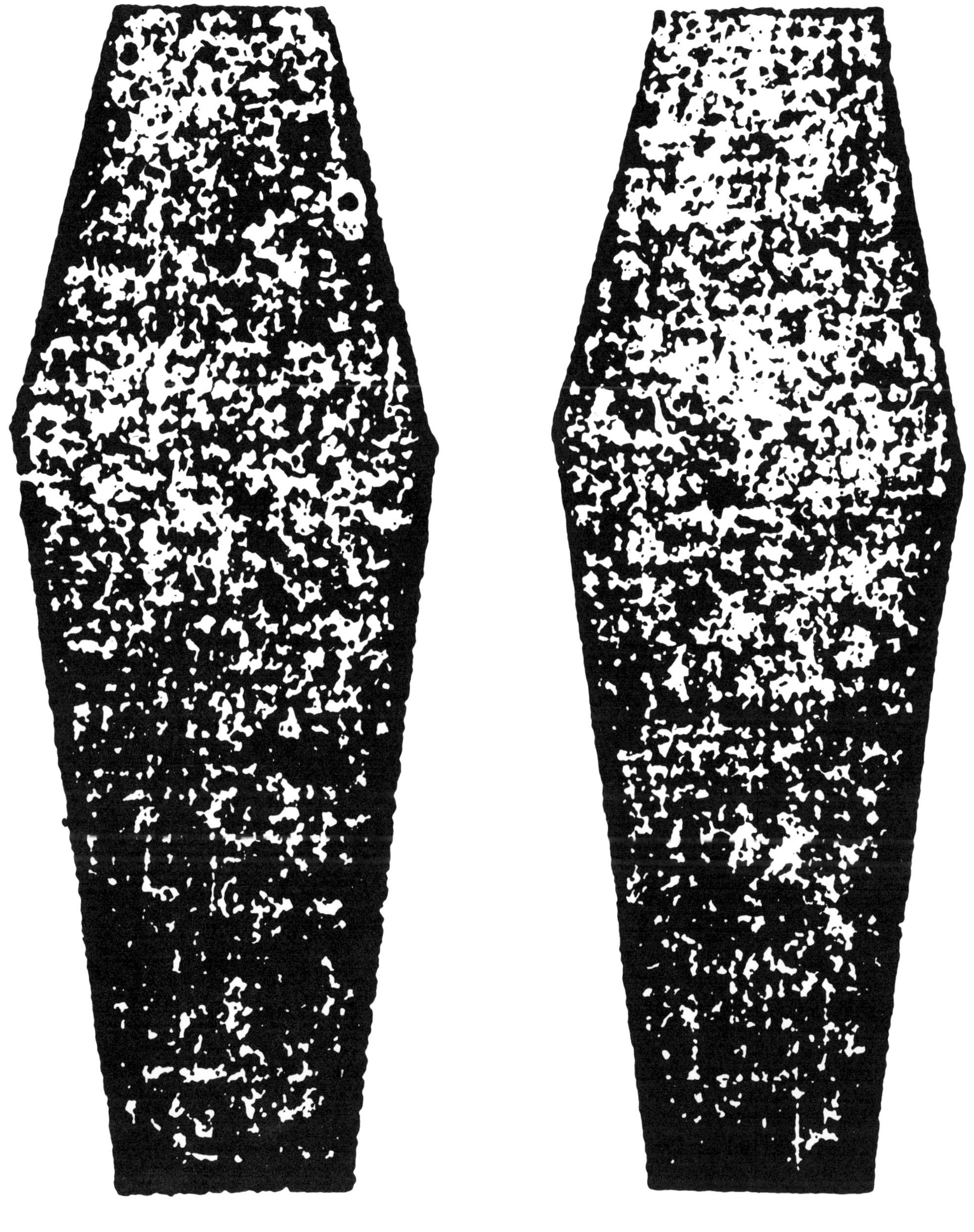

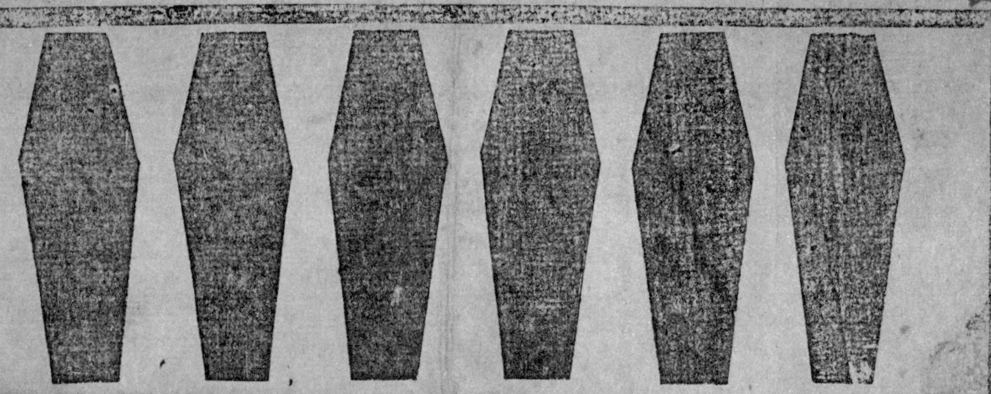

Serious Thoughts on ſudden Death.

A P O E M, occaſioned by the drowning of ſix men by the overſeting of a boat in Lake Champlain, near Split Rock, about twenty miles below Crown-Point. There were eight perſons in the boat when it overſet, but two ſaved their lives by keeping to the boat.

LORD how precarious are our lives,
Our fleeting years how ſwift they fly,
No earthly thing true pleaſure gives,
No ſoul-felt joy beneath the ſky.

Death, like an ever-rolling ſtream,
Advances on by ſwift degrees,
Our joys a mere deluſive dream,
Soon looſe the very power to pleaſe.

How many are the dreadful ſcenes,
In which Death ſhakes our mortal frame,
E'en life's beſt bleſſings are a means,
To ſend our ſouls to whence they came:

The forked lightning's fiery blaze,
The tempeſt's roaring on the ſea,
Whirlwinds and hurricanes prove ways,
From mortal life to ſet us free.

Hark 'tis a doleful ſolemn ſound,
That with ſuch horror ſtrikes the ear,
Ye northern realms attend the ſound,
The ſovereign ruler learn to fear.

Death has his dread appearance made,
In tempeſts ſhewn his mighty power,
Six mortals number'd with the dead,
Two only 'ſcap'd the fatal hour.

Contending elements engage,
With horrid ſounds they ſtrike the ear,
The rolling billows foam with rage,
The hardy boatmen quake with fear.

Tempeſts in dreadful order riſe,
Loud ſtormy winds with ratling hail,
Black clouds o'erſpread the low'ring ſkies,
The greateſt humanefforts fail.

The dreadful voice of heaven is heard,
In thundering accents from above,
Aſtoniſh'd mortals, unprepared,
Are ſummon'd to their laſt remove.

Their boat, ſo late their ſafe abode,
Swift gliding o'er the placid lake,
The ſwelling billows diſcommode,
In vain is all the care they take.

Now plung'd into the troubled deep,
In vain they ſpread their arms abroad,
Surviving mortals learn to weep,
Their fate and make your refuge God.

To God they lift their earneſt cry,
To him addreſs their ardent prayer,
Alas poor mortals [illegible] muſt die,
The end of human [illegible] draws near.

Oh may ſurvivors learn to live,
Each fleeting hour prepar'd to die,
Thus ſhould we ſolid joys receive,
Such joys as fill the world on high.

How muſt ſurviving friends be griev'd,
To hear the ſolemn tidings told,
Of deareſt relatives bereav'd,
In death's embraces ſtiff and cold.

No friends to lend a helping hand,
To ſave them overwhelm'd in grief,
To help their ſinking boat to land,
Or yield the much deſir'd relief.

Thus dreadful are the ways of God,
Thus ſudden are the ſtrokes of death,
His awful mandates fly abroad,
And mortals muſt reſign their breath.

Yet though our lives thus ſwiftly paſs,
How do the thoughtleſs guilty race,
Urge the ſwift ſand of nature's glaſs,
And ſcorn their maker to his face.

How many raſhly lift their hands,
Againſt the life which God has given,
Deſpiſing his ſupreme commands,
And ſcorning every rule of Heaven.

Great God beſtow thy grace and love,
Oh give us hearts to be ſincere,
Our doubts and wicked thoughts remove,
And make thy glorious power appear.

Jeſus thou great incarnate King,
Reclaim us to thy ſacred cauſe,
Let judgments reformation bring,
And make us bow unto thy laws.

Grant us a ſpirit fram'd to bear
The pains and trials of the croſs,
Fill us with love and holy fear,
And purge our ſouls from ſin and droſs.

NUMBER 1

THE first broadsides printed in Vermont usually informed citizens of actions taken by the Governor and Council or the Legislature. "Serious Thoughts on sudden Death" (1787) is the earliest example of an illustrated broadside treating a topic unrelated to government.

The printer, and perhaps author, Anthony Haswell of Bennington, came to Vermont in 1783. Born in Portsmouth, England, in 1756, he emigrated to America in 1770 and learned the printer's trade from Isaiah Thomas in Worcester, Massachusetts. After service in the Revolution and a few years of printing work in Hartford, Connecticut, and Springfield, Massachusetts, he finally moved to Bennington, where he published the *Vermont Gazette* with occasional interruptions from 1783 until his death in 1816.

First with David Russell and then Benjamin Smead as partners, Haswell directed a printing, publishing, and bookselling business which his sons Anthony J., David R., and William continued into the 1820s. William published *The Green Mountain Farmer* (1811–13) and later served as State Printer (1818–20).

Anthony Haswell was imprisoned for sixty days in 1800 under the Sedition Act. His now lost broadside, "Serious Thoughts on the Present Troubles in Massachusetts" (1787), perhaps also in verse like the broadside printed here, would be a useful document for tracing Haswell's political thinking from the time of Shays's Rebellion to his incarceration for publishing statements against the President "with the intent to defame" or bring him into "contempt or disrepute."

DATE: 1787

LOCATION: American Antiquarian Society

SIZE: 45.5 x 27.8 cm.

A POEM, compoſed on the Death of MR. STEPHEN BATCHELLER, *and* MR. DENISON GALLUP, *who were both drowned at Quechy Falls, in Connecticut River, on the 5th of Auguſt, 1805. Mr. Batcheler, who was in the twenty-fifth year of his age, had, not long before, been married to an amiable young woman, with whom he had lived but a few months, when he, in company with his Father, went to work at the place above mentioned, where he continued until the fatal day which terminated his exiſtence.*

1. HARK! hark! what ſad cries do I hear,
 That echo from ſhore unto ſhore,
Proclaiming, that BATCHELLER dear,
 And GALLUP, his friend, are no more!

2. How ſad, how diſtreſſing, the hour,
 To all the ſpectators around;
No help, or relief in their power;
 Their friends and companions are drown'd.

3. How thoughtleſs and heedleſs they go,
 Where dangers beſet them around,
Where billows are rolling below,
 And waters the rocks do ſurround.

4. Young GALLUP, his friend for to ſave,
 Ruſh'd into the dangers around;
There ſunk in the watery grave;
 No help for them either was found.

5. As young BATCHELLER ſinks in the wave,
 His Parent ſtands ſwelling with grief;
No arm, his dear Son, now can ſave,
 No mortal can give him relief.

6. He's gone, (the fond Parent he cries,)
 He ſinks in the watery deep;
Forever now hid from my eyes,
 His body ſhall quietly ſleep.

7. Adieu! deareſt Child, now adieu!
 Thy God, he hath call'd for thee home;
Though hard it is parting with you,
 You ſeem to make haſte to be gone.

8. What ſorrows attend my fond heart,
 Whilſt I the ſad tidings unfold!
For Mother and Son thus to part,
 Her ſorrows can never be told.

9. His Brothers and Siſters, likewiſe,
 With ſorrow ſhall hang down their head,
Say, STEPHEN, the prudent and wiſe,
 Lies ſilent and low, with the dead.

10. B[illegible]t hark, [illegible]e ſad news to relate,
 To [illegible] who [illegible]early alli'd,
His Par[illegible] Friend, and his Mate,
 So lately his beautiful Bride.

11. Her boſom, with ſorrow and ſighs,
 Is ready to burſt for relief;
But tears will not flow from her eyes;
 Her ſorrows forbid her to weep.

12. Her ſorrows at laſt find a vent;
 Her boſom ſtill throbbing with fears;
Her griefs that ſo long have been pent,
 Are flowing along with her tears.

13. He's gone, now this fair one, ſhe cries;
 His body ſhall quietly ſleep;
He, that once delighted my eyes,
 Has left me alone for to weep.

14. Soon, *Gabriel's* loud trumpet ſhall ſound,
 And bid my fair STEPHEN ariſe,
No longer to ſleep in the ground,
 But riſe to his God in the ſkies.

15. O! there ſhall I meet him again,
 In raptures of pleaſure and love;
Where, freed from all ſorrow and pain,
 We'll ſoar to the region above.

16. With cherubs and angels, we'll ſing,
 The love of [illegible] God, and his Son;
Thus [illegible] heavenly wing,
 Our praiſes [illegible] ſongs ſhall be one!

A POEM, compoſed on the Death of MR. DENISON GALLUP, who was drowned in *Connecticut River*, on the 5th of Auguſt, 1805, aged 28.

1. BEHOLD the roſy in its bloom,
Cut down and wither'd, ere 'tis noon:
So was this lovely Son of thine
Cut down, and periſh'd in his prime.

2. And left a mother fond and dear
Over his grave to ſhed the tear,
And mourn the loſs of this her Son,
Whoſe days were ſpent, his glaſs was run.

3. The elements did there conſpire,
To rob her of her fond deſire;
He ſinks into the watery wave,
Striving his drowning friend to ſave.

4. The weeping mother crown'd with years,
Her face is furrow'd with her tears,
Cries, Oh, he's gone, his ſpirit's fled,
My DENISON lies with the dead!

5. The aged Mother now draws near,
Over her Son to ſhed a tear,
To ſee his body laid in duſt,
But ſoon to walk amongſt the juſt.

6. The Brother there does weeping ſtand,
The Siſters, too, with joining hand,
With tears and lamentation, ſay,
Our deareſt Brother ſleeps in clay.

7. The mourning crowd do gather round,
To lay his body in the ground,
Where it ſhall reſt in mould'ring clay,
Until the great deciſive Day.

8. His active limbs are now at eaſe,
His uſeful tongue that once could pleaſe,
His ſparkling eye that ſhone ſo bright,
Is clos'd in everlaſting night.

9. But ſoon our Brother we ſhall meet,
In heavenly joys each other greet,
And ſing the joys of heavenly love,
In the bright kingdom that's above.

10. Upon that bright and golden ſhore,
Where ſighs and ſorrows are no more,
Where youth and beauty ne'er decay,
Where all is one eternal day.

11. When God ſhall wake his ſleeping duſt,
His earthly tomb he then ſhall burſt,
With ſongs of triumph, mount above,
And ſing redeeming grace and love.

12. Sleep then, ſweet youth, till that bright [morn,
When Chriſt your body ſhall adorn,
With his own likeneſs clear and bright,
Then mount to worlds of pureſt light.

13. All you who mourn this friend moſt [dear,
As o'er his grave you ſhed a tear,
Say, here lies DENISON at reſt,
Ye clods, lie lightly on his breaſt.

14. He once was active, briſk and brave,
He now lies mould'ring in this grave;
This is *his* lot, it ſoon is *mine*,
When I this vital breath reſign.

NUMBER 2

POOR Denison Gallup, drowned at 28, left many unhappy friends. Probate records in Windsor County show a claim on his estate for $330 from a group of thirteen men who lived in and around the village of Hartland. It is not known if any money owing to his companion Stephen Batcheller was forgiven at the fateful moment on August 5, 1805, when they were swept over the roaring waters of Queechee Falls.

DATE: 1805

LOCATION: Vermont Historical Society

SIZE: 39 x 16 cm.

A CHRISTMAS HYMN,

COMPOSED BY THE HON. *ROYALL TYLER*, CHIEF JUSTICE OF THE STATE OF VERMONT, AND SUNG AT CLAREMONT, *N. H.* 1793.

1. HAIL to the joyous day,
On which our Lord was born;
Lift high the vocal lay,
And sing the blissful morn.
Your voices raise!
To hail the morn
On which was born
The LORD of grace.

2. That sun which cheers the plains,
The seasons as they move,
Rich dews and fertile rains,
All prove his sovereign love.
Your voices raise!
To HIM who cheers,
The fruitful years,
Be grateful praise.

3. HE o'er the trackless waste
Our pious fathers led;
And though in desert plac'd,
He them with blessings fed:
Your voices raise!
To HIM who binds
The waves and winds,
Be endless praise.

4. HE crown'd fair freedom's cause;
He made our nation great;
The Leader of our wars
He raised to rule our States.
Your voices raise!
To HIM who brings
To earth proud kings,
Be deathless praise.

5. He taught us to discern
Blest Freedom's sacred plan;
And Europe's kingdom's learn
Of us the rights of man.
Your voices raise!
To HIM who broke
Oppression's yoke,
Be endless praise.

6. Where roam'd the savage race,
In cruelty and blood,
He form'd this sacred place,
A temple for our God.
Your voices raise,
Let earth resound,
The coral sound
Of sovereign grace.

7. Here where the savage foes,
Their deathful war-song sung;
Sweet peace her olive shows,
And joy on earth is sung.
Your voices raise!
Let all accord
To praise the Lord,
The Lord of grace.

8. When fell contagion cast
The gale of death around,
He turn'd the sickly blast,
And ruddy health we found.
Your voices raise!
To Christ the Son,
Who crowns his own
With length of days.

9. Has sorrow weigh'd us down,
He gave, when death was near,
A balm for ev'ry wound,
A joy for ev'ry tear.
Your voices raise!
To HIM who hears
The wretch's prayers,
Be endless praise.

10. Let solemn organs sound,
And sweeten cords combine,
Swell the full notes around,
With grateful voices join.
Your voices raise!
On every wing,
In transport sing
The Saviour's praise.

NUMBER 3

KNOWN mainly as the author of *The Contrast*, the first written and professionally produced stage comedy in the United States (1787), Royall Tyler (1757–1826) was a lawyer, militiaman (he helped quell Shays's Rebellion), journalist, novelist, poet, and chief justice of Vermont's Supreme Court (1807–13).

"A Christmas Hymn" was first sung at church services in Claremont, New Hampshire, in 1793. Published twice in that same year—first as a broadside and then in the Claremont *Eagle*—"A Christmas Hymn" is among the first of Tyler's works after moving to Vermont from Massachusetts. This issue of the broadside was published during Tyler's six-year service on Vermont's Supreme Court.

DATE: ca. 1810

LOCATION: Dartmouth College

SIZE: 25 x 20 cm.

LINES

WRITTEN BY LUCY WINN,

On the death of ABNER WRIGHT, of Whitingham,

WHO DIED JUNE 3d, 1812.

YE dying sons of men draw near,
A solemn call from God to hear,
His Providence calls loud on you,
Prepare to bid this world adieu.

When one doth die he calls on thee
To meet thy God prepared be,
For Christ the judge you soon must meet,
And stand before the judgment seat.

Behold a man in prime of Life,
With three young children and a wife;
He's left them on this Earthly clod,
Where is he gone? I trust to God.

Forty one years and some above
He did sojourn with us in love,
Till Jesus call'd him from below,
Through death's dark gloomy shade to go.

Consumption, seated near his heart,
Did prey upon his vital part,
It made his flesh and strength decay,
And took his precious life away.

When sickness did him first arrest,
About his soul he was distress'd
'Till Jesus by his matchless grace,
Display'd the brightness of his face.

God did his soul with comfort fill,
And sweet submisson to his will,
And even till his latest breath
Did triumph o'er the fear of death.

Never shall I forget that day,
I hear'd this man exhort and pray,
Sinners, he warned most faithfully
From God's avenging wrath to fly.

His joyful soul appeared bles'd
With joy that cannot be expres'd;
Glory to God! I hear'd him say,
Glory to Christ eternally.

O! had I Mountains here of gold,
And silver more than can be tol'd,
It would not tempt me here to stay,
I long to go, with Christ to be.

Farewell said he to neighbours here,
Farewell my tender partner dear;
You've nothing more for me to do,
Farewell my tender children too.

Don't hold me in this world below,
Resign me up and let me go,
Don't weep my spouse and break thy heart,
'Tis but a little while we part.

Soon death's last strugles will be o'er,
Then I shall sigh and grieve no more;
And then untill his latest breath
He sang a victory over death.

Come sinners now forewarned be,
Religion's a reallity,
Remember tho' he's out of sight,
You soon must meet with Abner Wright.

His solemn calls and every thought
Will into judgment then be brought,
O flee escape a burning hell,
That you in endless bliss may dwell.

O come and view the dying saint
Distress'd yet making no complaint;
Come saints admire and praise the grace,
For Jesus is a hiding place.

His widowed Friend with weeping ey s
Calls loud on us to sympathise,
Also an only Brother too;
My Soul would sympathise with you.

May she a widow be indeed,
And God from heaven supply her need;
Come saints to God lift fervent prayers
To take these children in his care.

His sister, also for him mourn,
But he must not to them return,
Submit to Christ, not long before
You'l meet with him, to part no more.

All flesh like grass does quickly fade,
And man beneath the ground is laid,
O may we then prepared be
To reign with Christ eternally.

NUMBER 4

ABNER Wright (1771–1812), of Whitingham in southern Vermont, died of consumption, the disease that swept like wildfire across Vermont in the first quarter of the nineteenth century and would have decimated the State had it not been for the increase in population through heavy migration from the turn of the century until the War of 1812.

Abner was also burned by the other fire that swept Vermont about the same time—the spiritual fire of evangelical revivals, one of which was doubtless the occasion for his conversion. Revivals, with their emphasis on personal salvation and communion with other Christians, instilled a new sense of worth in individuals like Wright, who, in a time of personal insecurity and national confusion, yearned for stability and order.

DATE: 1812

LOCATION: Vermont Historical Society

SIZE: 25.5 x 21 cm.

The Bold Lads of Canada.

COME all you British heroes, I pray you lend an ear—
Draw up your British forces, and then your volunteers—
We're going to fight the Yankee-boys, by water and by land,
And we never will return until we conquer, sword in hand—
We're the noble lads of Canada—come to arms, boys, come.

O! now the time has come, my boys, to cross the Yankees' line—
We remember they were rebels once, and conquered John Burgoyne.
We'll subdue those haughty Democrats, and pull their dwellings down,
And we'll have the States inhabited with subjects to the crown—
We're the noble lads, &c.

We've as choice a British army as ever cross'd the seas—
We'll burn both town and city, and with smoke becloud the skies;
We'll subdue the old *Green Mountain boys*, their Washington is gone,
And we'll play them *Yankee Doodle*, as the Yankees did Burgoyne.
We're the noble lads, &c.

Now we've reach'd the Plattsb'gh banks my boys and here we'll make a stand
Until we take the yankee fleet McDonough doth command;
We've the Growler and the Eagle, that from Smith we took away;
And we'll have their noble fleet that lies anchor'd in the bay—
We're the noble lads, &c.

O! our fleet is hove in view, my boys, the cannons loudly roar,
With death upon our cannon balls, we'll drench their decks with gore,
We've a water craft sufficient for to sink them in an hour;
But our orders are to board, and the Yankee's flag destroy.
We're the noble lads, &c.

O! what bitter groans and sighing we heard on board the fleet,
While McDonough's cocks are crowing boys I fear we shall get beat;
If we lose the cause by sea, my boys, we'll make a quick return,
For as sure as hell is hell we shall all be Burgoyn'd,
We're the noble lads of Canada—stand at arms, boys, stand.

Now the battles' growing hot, my boys, I dont know how 'twill turn,
While McDonough's boats on swivels hung continually to burn—
We see such constant flashing that the smoke beclouds the day,
And our larger boats they've struck, and our smaller run away.
O we've got too far from Canada—run for life, boys, run.

O! Provost he sigh'd aloud, and to his officers he said
"I wish the Devil and those Yankees could but sail along side—
"For the tars of France and England can't stand before them well,
"For I think they'd flog the devils and drive them back to hell."
O we've got to far, &c.

Now prepare for your retreat, my boys, make all the speed you can,
The Yankees are surrounding us, we'll surely be Burgoyn'd—
Behind the hedges and the ditches and the trees and every stump
You can see the sons of bitches and the cursed Yankees jump.
O we've got too far, &c.

Now we've reach'd the Chazy heights, my boys we'll make a short delay,
For to rest our weary limbs, and to feed our beasts on hay—
Soon McDonoughs cocks began to crow, 'was heard at Starks' barn,
And a report throughout the camp was the general alarm,
O we've got too far, &c.

O! Provost he sigh'd aloud, and to his officers did say,
"The yankee troops are hove in sight and hell will be to pay:
"Shall we fight like men of courage and do the best we can,
"When we know they will flog us two to one? I think we'd better run.
"O we've got too far, &c."

Now if ever I reach Quebec alive I'll surely stay at home,
For McDonough's gain'd the victory, the Devil fight McComb—
I had rather fight a thousand troops as good as e'er cross'd the seas
Than fifty of those Yankee Boys behind the stumps and trees.
O we've got too far, &c.

They told us that the Federalists were friendly to the Crown;
They'd join our Royal Army and the Democrats pull down;
But they all unite together as a band of brothers join'd;
They will fight for Independence till they die upon the ground.
O we've got too far, &c.

The Old 76's have sallied forth, upon their crutches they do lean;
With their rifles level'd on us, with their spect's they take good aim;
For there's no retreat to those, my boys, who'd rather die than run;
And we make no doubt but these are those that conquer'd John Burgoyne,
When he got too far, &c.

Now we've reach'd the British ground, my boys we'll have a day of rest—
And I wish my soul that I could say 'twould be a day of mirth—
But I've left so many troops behind, it causes me to mourn—
And if ever I fight the Yankees more I'll surely stay at home.
Now we've all got back to Canada—stay at home, boys, stay.

Here's a health to all the British troops, likewise to George Provost;
And to our respective families, and the girls that love us most—
To McDonough and M'Comb and to every Yankee Boy—
Now fill up your tumblers full, for I never was so dry.
Now we've all got back to Canada—stay at home, boys, stay.

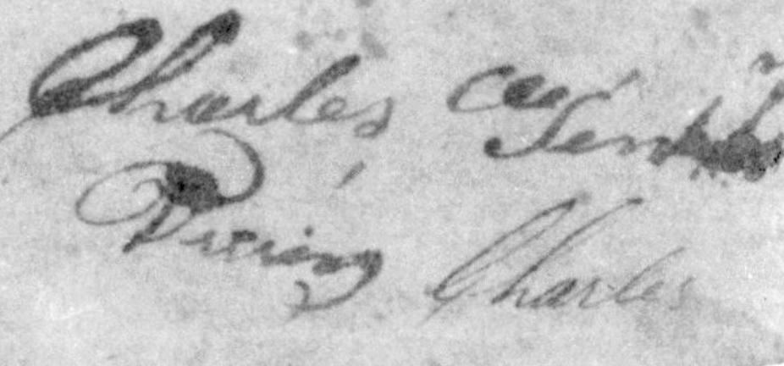

NUMBER 5

THE classic route of invasion from the St. Lawrence Valley to the Hudson River and New York was up Lake Champlain. Like the Indians, the French, and Burgoyne before him, the British General Sir George Prevost in 1814 led the finest army ever sent to North America against American regulars and militia on and around the lake. Prevost's army of 10,000 met fewer than 3,000 men at Plattsburgh on the New York side of Champlain. On September 11 the British and American fleets of small vessels, mostly without bulwarks to protect their crews, engaged in a murderous conflict in which, despite the loss of one fifth of his crew, the American Captain Macdonough managed to turn his ship completely around at anchor and force the surrender of the British flagship, *Confiance*, and three other vessels. Prevost, who had failed to take the small but strongly fortified American positions at the south end of Plattsburgh Bay, retreated in discouragement to Canada.

DATE: 1814

LOCATION: Vermont Historical Society

SIZE: 29.75 x 23.5 cm.

A wonderful DREAM,

By Dr. Isaac Watts, author of the Psalms and Hymns so highly esteemed by Christians of all denominations.

WHEN the bright monarch of the day
  Withdrew from human sight,
And night had spread her sable veil,
  And put the day to flight;
Then slumber seiz'd my closing eyes,
  My weary limbs repose,
While to my soul with vast surprize,
  This wondrous VISION rose.
Struck pale and low my body lay,
  A lifeless lump of clay,
And people solemnly advanc'd
  To bear my corpse away.
As the procession shap'd its way,
  Lo! from the crystal skies,
Swift shot away an angel forth,
  And stood before my eyes.
Swiftly he bore me by the hand,
  Through the etherial blue,
Leaving the lesser orbs of light,
  And higher planets too.
The earth, the clouds, the moon and stars
  In distant view decay:
Thro' liquid realms and starry plains
  He urg'd his shining way,
Curious, I ask'd my lovely guide,
  As through the spheres we past,
Concerning all those beauteous scenes
  Which by us fled so fast.
Silent he check'd my forward tongue,
  Nor staid to make reply,
Still rising with angelic speed,
  To tread the upper sky.
Now all at once before my eyes
  A blooming garden rose;
Here ancient Eden's flow'ry walks
  Their endless greens disclose.
Up a tall hill my footsteps rise,
  Which in the linten swells,
Around with various curious dyes
  The flowers adorn'd the vales
The waving trees with pressing buds
  Crowd into living groves,
Thro' whose fair boughs with cheerful songs
  The feather'd nation roves.
Tid upward as I point my sight
  I saw with vast surprize.
Thy shining spires, JERUSALEM,
  And blazing temple rise.
Ten thousand beauties charm my breast,
  While still my eyes behold
Thy glittering walls and fiery gates,
  And lofty towers of gold.
The shining seraph led my way
  Through the etherial blue,
Yet the illustrious door appear'd
  Still glit'ring in my view.
And mounting up from sphere to sphere,
  With my angelic guigle,
At length, methought, at distance I
  A monstrous shape espy'd,
Stalking across the spacious plain,
  Which lay at my right hand,
To which I came, while at the last
  My lofty guide did stand.
Sure 'tis the black infernal prince,
  Thought I, to whom I said,
Proudest of rebels, who did once
  Heav'n's mighty realms invade:
Thou monarch of malicious fiends,
  And of the pit below!
What dost thou on this heavenly plain
  And whither dost thou go?
[illegible]
  For sins surprising red,
Before the awful bar of GOD,
  You'll presently be had.
Where, from the glorious Judge's mouth,
  Thy sentence will proceed,
Whose piercing sound will make thy heart
  Tho hard as steel to bleed
Then thou'lt be bound both hand and foot,
  With adamantine chains.
And then I'll drag thee down to hell,
  To bear eternal pains.
This is the reason why I left
  The horrid shades of night,
And to these fair celestial plains
  Did take my lofty flight.
He also said, on Sabbath day,
  Before the sun resign'd
The spacious skies to sable night,
  To gratify your mind,
You walk'd abroad to such an house,
  With one that I did send
To tempt you to profane that day,
  Which you did not intend.
Thus, you I tempted oft you'll find,
  Against the mighty GOD;
Your bold rebellion now demands
  His sin-revenging rod.
Whilst dreaming thus my restless mind
  Was sorely pressed with these,
My conscience smote me and my guilt
  Did on my spirits seize.
Then to the hateful prince of hell,
  With trembling I reply'd,
'Tis true I have provok'd my GOD,
  But JESUS CHRIST has dy'd
To save the humble simple soul
  From hell's incessant pains,
And he will keep my soul secure
  From your infernal chains.
Then did the apostate stalk away
  Some distance from my side,
And tow'rds the famous city he
  With monstrous steps did stride.
And then the angel led me on,
  With looks surprizing sweet,
Treading the pure celestial plain
  With his immortal feet.
Then o'er the blest immortal field,
  With swiftness he did pass,
And reach'd the glorious city wall,
  Which seem'd like crystal glass.
There stately gates of precious pearls
  Adorn'd the beauteous side,
To which transported I was led
  By my celestial guide.
Then two of those resplendent pearls,
  Which turn'd on rubies bright,
Open'd inviting my approach,
  O'er-whelm'd with vast delight.
And then the angel led me on
  With his most tender hand,
And led me to an awful bar,
  Where near the Judge did stand.
Before a lofty shining throne
  Of bright celestial gold,
On adamantine pillars rais'd,
  Most glorious to behold.
On this the blessed JESUS sat,
  The FATHER's chief delight,
Cloath'd with a long unspotted robe,
  Like snow unsullied white.
I also saw ten thousand saints
  Around his burning throne,
And tuneful angels sounding loud
  The victories he had won.
The saints in spotless garments clad,
  Did sing with joys supreme,
The FATHER, SON, and HOLY GHOST,
  Was their eternal theme.
The sacred anthems from their tongues
  Flow'd to their SAVIOUR's praise,
While I stood mute before the throne,
  Borne down with vast amaze.
Such dismal terrors seiz'd my soul,
  Such shame spread o'er my face,
That then I could no bear to see
  The glories of the place.
Then did the holy righteous Judge,
  The cause of me enquire,
Why I stood trembling at the bar,
  And what I did desire?
Then I reply'd, to hear my doom
  Pronounc'd, I now appear:
Then JESUS with gracious smile,
  My fainting soul did cheer.
And taking up a pond'rous book,
  Wrote by the eternal pen,
Whose faithful pages did contain
  The fates of mortal men;
He did unfold the numerous leaves,
  With his immortal hand,
Before the blest melodious crowd,
  Which round the throne did stand.
There I observ'd while pages wrote
  With never-failing red,
While over others I beheld
  Black characters were spread.
Then said the Judge, the scarlet lines
  Contain the names of those
For whom I shed my dearest blood,
  And whom my father chose
Before he made the darksome night
  Or ever day did dawn,
And for that reason here they stand
  In rosy scarlet drawn.
And in this list of blessed souls
  I also set thy name,
Before this hand spread out the sky,
  Or form'd earth's morning frame.
And then he added with a look
  Which made my heart rejoice,
Could ought in thee commend thyself
  As worthy of my choice.
When I did pass by other souls
  And set my love on thee?
To which transported I reply'd,
  'Twas nothing, Lord, in me.
My soul was filled with boundless joy,
  For then I call'd to mind,
How I that very day had read
  Concerning human kind;
That the delight of JESUS was
  Among the race of man,
Who were by him exalted high,
  Before the world began.
Then ceas'd the glorious judge to speak
  Who never spoke amiss,
At which my convoy turn'd to go
  Among the saints in bliss.
And I, methought, wrapt up in joy,
  Did also turn aside,
To join the blest harmonious throng,
  With my celestial guide.
And then the ever blessed Judge,
  The Lamb that once was slain,
Said, yet you must not enter there,
  But must return again,
And live on earth from whence you came,
  And fight the glorious fight,
Against the devil, world and sin,
  And put them all to flight.
For I will grant the grace of faith,
  That bright immortal shield,
And other prov'd celestial arms
  [illegible]
Then turning from the sapphire throne,
  I saw the prince of hell,
To whom I said, Thou hateful fiend,
  Thou dragon fierce and fell!
Thy vile deceit and cursed spite
  Was seen, when by a wile,
Thou didst in Eden's sacred grove
  Our mother Eve beguile.
Then with a hideous voice he said,
  Your hope of grace is vain,
For I will surely win your soul,
  By tempting you again.
Then I reply'd, I fear you not,
  The Prince of Life has said,
That his almighty sovereign grace
  Shall surely be my aid.
At which, with envy, spite and rage,
  His furious breast was swell'd,
And with his wide distended jaws
  The frightful monster yell'd.
And straddling widely o'er the plain,
  He reach'd the adverse side
Of the blest hill, to that which I
  Ascended with my guide.
Where with impetuous fury he
  Tore up the trembling ground,
And with his dismal cloven paws
  Did throw the clods around.
Then with a mild seraphic mein
  The angel did retreat,
Leading me from the awful bar,
  And from the judgement seat.
Descending with me through the skies
  The way we came before,
He brought me safely to the earth,
  And set me at my door,
Where we engag'd in sweet discourse
  About the great unknown,
And of the glories of the saints
  That stand around the throne,
But in the midst of our discourse
  I suddenly awoke,
So to my grief the dream dissolv'd,
  And the sweet vision broke.

PRINTED AT WOODSTOCK.—1821.

NUMBER 6

ISAAC Watts (1674–1748), the English hymn writer and author of "O God, our help in ages past," was the most frequently published foreign author in Vermont up to at least 1820. No other single author of hymns or religious treatises approached the popularity of the twenty-four editions of his *Psalms, Hymns, and Spiritual Songs Applied to the Christian State of Worship* (Middlebury, 1814), *The Psalms of David* (Monteplier, 1814), and *The Improvement of the Mind* (Bennington, 1817). Among secular authors only Noah Webster was comparable in the number of his books published in Vermont.

DATE: 1821

LOCATION: Vermont Historical Society

SIZE: 44.5 x 24 cm.

Inventions, Discoveries, & Public Announcements

STOP THIEF!

STOLEN From the Subscriber, in *Pittsfield*, on Friday Night last, a bay HORSE, 7 or 8 Years old, near 15 Hands high, has a dark Mane and Tail, trots and paces, carries himself well, was shod before, and somewhat low in flesh.——Whoever will take up the said Horse and Thief, and secure the Thief so that he may be brought to Justice, and give Information to the Subscriber, shall be handsomely rewarded, and all necessary Charges paid by CHARLES GOODRICH.

Pittsfield, June 29, 1789.

N. B. A Saddle and Bridle was stolen at the same Time.——The Saddle had a quilted Deer-skin Seat, and blue Cloth Housing, both considerably worn.

A L S O,

STOLEN The same Night, from ZADOCK HUBBARD, in said *Pittsfield*, a dark roan HORSE, 11 or 12 Years old, rising 14 Hands high, his Face some scarrified, trots and paces, one hind Hoof split, shod before, was some marked with Geers on his Sides, and it is supposed was taken away with a Curb Bridle with a single Rein.——Whoever will take up said Horse and Thief, and secure the Thief so that he may be brought to Justice, shall have TEN DOLLARS Reward, or FIVE DOLLARS for the Horse only, and all necessary Charges paid by ZADOCK HUBBARD.

Pittsfield, June 29, 1789.

NUMBER 7

HORSELESS Charles Goodrich and Zadock Hubbard (or the unknown printers of this broadside) not only knew the value of their stolen horses, but also knew that a shout in print, if widely posted—with promise of a handsome reward (the thief was worth as much as the horse to Hubbard)—would be likely to get results. The directness of the title of this broadside and the emphasis on the criminal act would have been likely to secure attention.

DATE: 1789

LOCATION: Shelburne Museum

SIZE: 21 x 17.5 cm.

Reparation Lottery:

CLASS THE FIRST.

SCHEME.

THIS Lottery conſiſts of three thouſand tickets, to be ſold at two dollars each—amounting in the whole to ſix thouſand dollars.

Prizes.		Dollars.		Dollars.
1	of	1000	is	1000
2		300		600
1		100		100
4		50		200
2		40		80
5		20		100
10		10		100
20		6		120
120		5		600
350		4		1400
First number drawn,				50
Laſt number drawn,				50
				4400 Dollars

The fortunate poſſeſſor of the firſt number drawn, if a blank, will be entitled to fifty dollars, if a prize fifty dollars in addition to ſuch prize—and ſo alſo will the poſſeſſor of the laſt number drawn.

A liſt of the fortunate numbers will be publiſhed in the public newſpapers, immediately after the drawing, and a copy of them lodged with the perſons who are entruſted by the managers with the ſale of tickets.

All prizes not applied for within ſix months after the publication of the prizes, ſhall be deemed forfeited to the uſe of the lottery.

All prizes of four dollars, if applied for within the above ſix months, ſhall be paid in tickets in the ſecond claſs of this lottery.

To the generous public.

AS the motives of the honorable General Aſſembly to grant this lottery, are well known to have ariſen from their patriotic deſire to encourage the beneficial manufacture of brandies, ſtrong beer, &c. in this ſtate, as well as to raiſe up a diſtreſſed, unfortuuate, worthy fellow citizen, ſo the managers flatter themſelves, that thoſe who love their country, as well as thoſe who love to ſuccour the diſtreſſed, will join to promote a rapid ſale of the tickets.

As the prizes are very high for the number of the tickets, the fortunate will meet a preſent recompence, and even the unfortunate will have the conſciouſneſs of having done good, *and may the bleſſing of him who is ready to periſh fall upon them.*

The time of drawing, which it is expected will be in the month of February next, will be announced in the public papers.

N. B. Tickets to be paid for and the prizes paid out in ſilver or gold.

SAMUEL MILLER,
TIMOTHY OLCOTT,
MARTIN CHITTENDEN. } Managers,

RUTLAND, October 31, 1792.

NUMBER 8

LOTTERIES were a favored method of raising money for public purposes in the late eighteenth and early nineteenth centuries. Churches, roads, and bridges were built, loss by fire repaired, and the State debt paid by lottery.

Between 1783 and 1806 the State of Vermont ran at least twenty-five lotteries by Acts of the General Assembly. Many more were authorized through private bills introduced in the legislature by representatives from various parts of the State. Towns ran lotteries even more frequently than the State, however, as in the case of Readsboro, where a lottery was authorized in the 1780's to raise £150 by lottery to build a bridge over the Deerfield River. In the case of the lottery advertised by this broadside in 1792, the managers claimed the revenue would be spent to establish a distillery, a venture that accorded with the "patriotic desire" of the General Assembly.

DATE: 1792

LOCATION: Vermont Historical Society

SIZE: 27 x 16 cm.

HUBBEL'S NEW-INVENTED
WATER WHEEL,
FOR CORN MILLS.

(Secured by Letters Patent from the President of the United States.)

The subscriber having purchased of the original inventor, Mr. EPHRAIM HUBBEL, the privilege of making, constructing, using, and vending to others the right of making, constructing, and using the said WATER WHEEL, in any place within the County of Rutland, offers the same for sale, to those who may be disposed to purchase.

The superior advantages which this Wheel combines, above any other hitherto in use, will be sufficient to recommend it to Mill-Owners, in every part of the Country. This Wheel is applied to a perpendicular shaft, requires no geers, and, with a head and fall of 12 feet, may be turned at the rate of 160 revolutions in one minute of time: this motion, too, may be given with three fifths of the quantity of water necessary to carry other Wheels of the most improved kind; and, although it be covered within ten inches of the top, by back water, its motion will not be perceptibly impeded. A column of water twelve inches by three and a half, is as much as the Wheel requires, to give it the greatest velocity and strength. The greatest diameter of this Wheel, if applied to Corn Mills, is three feet six inches; it is not liable to freeze, with proper attention; and, where there is a low head and fall of water, may be charged on two sides, which will give it a sufficient motion. This Wheel greatly diminishes the expence of Mill building, and facilitates the operation of grinding beyond any other application.

Those who wish to see the above Wheel in operation, may call at Mr. JOHN REYNOLDS' Mills, in Rutland, or at Esq. CONANT'S, in Brandon.

Privileges will be disposed of, for single Wheels, or for whole towns, as may best suit the purchaser.

JESSE GOVE.

Rutland, 3d November, 1806.

NUMBER 9

For a part of New England that was still very much frontier settlements and scattered small farm holdings, Vermont obtained a surprisingly large number of patents during the first forty years of the Republic. By 1830 eleven patents for various kinds of mills had been granted by the federal government to Vermonters, one of which was to Ephraim Hubbel of Middlebury in May 1806.

More significantly, perhaps, thirty-four of the one hundred and twenty-two patents obtained by Vermonters in the same period were for various kinds of factory machinery. With only nineteen granted in those forty years, agriculture was a modest third in the list of enterprises impelling Yankee inventiveness in the boom period of Vermont's heaviest settlement before the War of 1812. Patents in the fine arts were granted for a spring-pen ruler and a method of teaching "the art of writing by lead plummet" (1812).

DATE: 1806

LOCATION: Vermont Historical Society

SIZE: 39 x 33 cm.

Military Announcements

Probably printed at Middlebury by Saml. Swift. (Sumner Papers)

BY HIS EXCELLENCY

MARTIN CHITTENDEN, Esquire,

GOVERNOR, CAPTAIN-GENERAL, AND COMMANDER IN CHIEF, IN AND OVER THE STATE OF VERMONT,

A PROCLAMATION:

***Whereas*, it appears, that the Third Brigade of** *the Third Division of the Militia of this State, has been ordered from our frontiers to the defence of a neighbouring State :—And, whereas it further appears, to the extreme regret of the Captain General, that a part of the Militia of said Brigade have been placed under the command, and at the disposal, of an Officer of the United States, out of the jurisdiction or control of the Executive of this State, and have been actually marched to the defence of a sister State, fully competent to all the purposes of self defence, whereby an extensive section of our own Frontier is left, in a measure, unprotected, and the peaceable, good citizens thereof are put in great jeopardy, and exposed to the retaliatory incursions and ravages of an exasperated enemy :—And, whereas, disturbances, of a very serious nature, are believed to exist, in consequence of a portion of the Militia having been thus ordered out of the State :—*

***Therefore*....to the end, that these great evils** may be provided against, and, as far as may be, prevented for the future :—

***Be it Known*....that such portion of the Mili-**tia of said Third Brigade, in said Third Divi[illegible] be now doing duty, in the State of New york, or else-where, beyond the limits of this State, both Officers and men, are hereby ordered and directed, by the Captain General and Commander in Chief of the Militia of the State of Vermont, forthwith to return to the respective places of their usual residence, within the territorial limits of said Brigade, and there to hold themselves in constant readiness to act, in obedience to the Orders of Brigadier General Jacob Davis, who is appointed, by the Legislature of this State, to the command of said Brigade.

And the said Brigadier General Davis is hereby ordered and directed, forthwith, to see, that the Militia of his said Brigade be completely armed and equipped, as the Law directs, and holden in constant readiness to march on the shortest notice, to the defence of the Frontiers; and, in case of actual invasion, without further Orders, to march with his said Brigade, to act, either in co-operation with the Troops of the United States, or separately, as circumstances may require, in repelling the enemy from our territory, and in protecting the good citizens of this State from their ravages or hostile incursions.

And in case of an event, so seriously to be deprecated, it is hoped and expected, that every citizen, without distinction of party, will fly at once to the nearest post of danger, and that the only rallying word will be—" OUR COUNTRY."

Feeling, as the Captain General does, the weight of responsibility, which rests upon him, with regard to the Constitutional duties of the Militia, and the sacred rights of our citizens to protection from this great class of community, so essentially necessary in all free countries; at a moment too, when they are so imminently exposed to the dangers of hostile incursions, and domestic difficulties, he cannot conscientiously discharge the trust reposed in him by the voice of his fellow citizens, and by the Constitution of this and the United States, without an unequivocal declaration, that, in his opinion, the Military strength and resources of this State, must be reserved for its own defence and protection, *exclusively*—excepting in cases provided for, by the Constitution of the United States; and then, under orders derived *only* from the Commander in Chief.

Given under my hand at Montpelier, this 10th day of November, in the year of our Lord One Thousand Eight Hundred and Thirteen; and of the Independence of the United States, the thirty eighth.

MARTIN CHITTENDEN.

BY HIS EXCELLENCY'S COMMAND,

SAMUEL SWIFT, *Secretary.*

GOVERNOR of Vermont from 1813 to 1815, Martin Chittenden (1763–1840), with many of his fellow Vermonters who voted Federalist against President James Madison, was opposed to the War of 1812. The Third Brigade of Vermont's Third Militia Division was ordered across Lake Champlain into New York early in September 1813, to join General Wade Hampton's ill-fated expedition against Canada, only to be thwarted by Canadian forces a few miles north of Plattsburgh at Chazy and Chateaugay in late September and October. Chittenden quickly proclaimed the deactivation of the brigade and ordered its return to Vermont. From their camp at Plattsburgh the officers responded: "we shall not obey your Excellency's order for returning, but shall continue in the service of our country."

DATE: 1813

LOCATION: Vermont Historical Society

SIZE: 29.5 x 18.5 cm.

NORTHERN SENTINEL, EXTRA.

BURLINGTON, Tueſday, September 13, 1814.

GLORIOUS INTELLIGENCE.

The anxiety of the public to learn the particulars of the late ſplendid victory over the Britiſh ſquadron on this Lake, has induced us to publiſh the following, which are all that have come to our knowledge.

On Sunday the ever memorable 11th of September, the enemy's ſquadron was diſcovered about eight o'clock, A. M. ſtanding up the lake with a favorable breeze, under a preſs of ſail. Every preparation was made by our gallant Commodore to give them a warm and cordial reception; with his ſquadron at anchor he awaited their approach. The enemy ſoon made their appearance off Cumberland Head and bore down for our ſquadron—the enemy's two largeſt veſſels taking a poſition to attack the Saratoga, our flag ſhip.—The firſt broadſide from her killed the Britiſh Commodore, (Downey,) and her fire continued ſo ſpirited and well directed that the enemy's flag ſhip, the Confiance ſoon after ſtruck. At this time the whole broad ſide guns of the Saratoga, next to the enemy, were completely unmanageable. The enemy's brig continued her fire. Our Commodore ſlipped his cable and wore round, two broadſides compelled the brig to follow the example of the Confiance—In the mean time the Preble compelled one the of enemy's ſloops to ſtrike. The other grounded on Hoſpital Iſland juſt before the battle ended, and was taken poſſeſſion of by ſome of our Gallies. The enemy's Gallies, except two which were ſunk, with the aſſiſtance of their oars, effected their eſcape. The ſlaughter on board the Britiſh fleet was immenſe. The Confiance alone had 190 killed. One of the captured ſloops had but five men alive. Our loſs is ſevere—60 men killed on board the Saratoga, & every officer except two midſhipmen were either killed or wounded—Commodore Macdonough himſelf was three different times knocked down by the ſplinters and falling ſpars and blocks, but has eſcaped with trifling injury. The loſs on either ſide it is difficult and as yet impoſſible to aſcertain.

The comparative loſs of the enemy with ours is ſtated at three to one. The number of priſoners is eſtimated at 6 or 700.

The Britiſh fleet conſiſted of nineteen veſſels, viz:

The Confiance, mounting	37 long 24's, S. locks,
Linnet,	22
Chub,	11
Finch,	11
10 Gallies, 2 each,	20
6 do. 1 do.	6
	108 guns.

Our fleet of fourteen veſſels, viz:

Saratoga,	28
Ticontaroga,	22
Warrior,	18
Com. Preble,	10
6 Gallies, 2 each,	12
4 do. 1 do.	4
	94

On the reſult of this moſt glorious victory comment is unneceſſary. The names of Macdonough and of his gallant officers, will be inſerted among thoſe of Decatur, Hull, Perry, Bainbridge, Porter and Jones, and like them will be held in everlaſting remembrance.

The enemy under Sir George Prevoſt amounting to 15000 regulars and embodied militia, in four brigades commanded by Major Generals De Rottenburgh, Powers, Briſbane and Robinſon, appeared before our works at Plattſburgh, and after bombarding, cannonading and rocket firing were oblieged to retreat in the night of Sunday laſt, in great confuſion, leaving a number of their tents, ſeveral pieces of cannon, great quantities of amunition, bombs, cannon-balls, grape ſhot, fixed cartridges, ſhovels, ſpades, axes, pick axes, bread, flower, beef, &c. &c. in our poſſeſſion, together with all their ſick and wounded to our mercy. The gallantry of General Macomb, his ſubalterns, and brave regulars, (not exceeding 1500) have never been exceeded. Not a pallid cheek was ſeen during the whole affair, notwithſtaning the ſhowers of ſhot, ſhells and rockets which were directed at our works. On ſilencing the enemy's battery the ſecond time, Sir George made his eſcape with his life guard, while we were playing the tune of Yankee Doodle.

The militia, nineteen thouſand, without diſtinction of party or age, in every inſtance have diſtinguiſhed themſelves.—The Vermont volunteers have behaved with the coolneſs of regulars, and their conduct has fulfiled the expectations, which the promptneſs and ſpirit with which they turned out had raiſed.

The enemy in their flight deſtroyed all the bridges and obſtructed the road by trees, baggage &c. They were however purſued as far as Chazy, but on account of the obſtructions of the road and their precipitant retreat, our *heroes* were not able to overtake them. The enemy have learnt a leſſon long to be remembered, that the "ſoil of Freedom is ſacred, that it muſt not, ſhall not, be polluted with impunity." In this their expedition by land and water, we can account to Sir George for more than *two thouſand* of his men killed and priſoners, and more than *ninety* pieces of cannon.

To the interpoſition of heaven, be aſcribed our glorious victory.

Our village laſt evening preſented a moſt brilliant ſpectacle. Every houſe was illuminated, which with the ringing of bells, diſcharges of muſketry, and ſalutes of ordnance from the wharf and encampment, proclaimed the joy of our citizens and their gratitude to their heroic deliverers.

Among the Vermont Volunteers, returning home from the purſuit of Sir Geore Prevoſt and his flying "conquerers of the veterans of France," was a venerable old man, one of the patriots of the Revolution, who upon leaving this town exclaimed in the language of ſcripture, "*Now, O Lord, let thy ſervant depart in peace, for mine eyes have ſeen thy ſalvation.*"

POSTSCRIPT.

Wedneſday morning, Sept. 14.

Intelligence has juſt arrived, giving the heart-cheering intelligence of the capture of 400 of the enemy's rear guard.

NUMBER 11

CAPTAIN Thomas Macdonough's defeat of the British at the naval battle of Plattsburgh was a decisive victory for American forces. With little for the new country to brag of after two years of "Mr. Madison's War," the surrender of the British flotilla and the death of its commodore off Cumberland Head on the west shore of Lake Champlain provided much needed encouragement for New England and a nation still shocked by the news of British officers occupying the White House and eating a dinner prepared for the fleeing President and Mrs. Madison.

The Northern Sentinel, founded in 1801 as the *Vermont Centinel*, was published in Burlington by Samuel Mills throughout the Embargo Era and the War of 1812, when it circulated news of Macdonough's victory at Plattsburgh Bay. In 1812 Mills's brothers, Ephraim and Thomas, assumed proprietorship of the paper, which ran until 1820. Thereafter the firm of E. & T. Mills, which continued well into the 1840's, printed books, including scholarly and philosophical texts for the faculty of the University of Vermont.

DATE: 1814

LOCATION: Vermont Historical Society

SIZE: 35 x 17 cm.

American Sentinel.

Yankee General, calling for Volunteers by sounding the Trumpet.

Gen. *Drummond* attempts to escape by the fleetness of a Bear, but is surrounded & taken prisoner.

General *Brisbane*, on a quick retreat, in imitation of a Monkey on a Pig.

A Cossack, smoaking his pipe & thumping his Mule with a cudgel to keep up with the rest.

A French Canadian, retreating on an Ass, & whipping up for dear life.

A Green-Mountain Boy, with his foot on the head of an Indian.

The feeling Matron follows her husband to the field of battle, to avenge the murders, flames and cruelties at Hampton, Havre-de-Grace, and the River Rasin!

The news of Champlain
The Prince Regent receives;
He mounts his old Bull,
To his tail he doth pull,
And, frantic with madness,
Most bitterly grieves.

THE

RETREAT

OF THE ENGLISH FROM

New-Orleans.

[A YANKEE SONG.]

THE *English* mustered mighty strong,
And hadn't their choicest troops along,
And thought it but a little song,
To take our town of Orleans.

From *Plymouth* and the *Chesapeake*,
From *Portsmouth* too, and *Cork*, so sleek,
All came to take a *Christmas* freak
In our gay town of Orleans.

Sir *Cochrane*, who is still'd *Sir Knight*,
With *Gordon* too, that naval wight,
And *Packenham*, all full of fight,
To have a dash at Orleans.

With *Gibbs* and *Keane* and *Lambert* too,
And others, who kept out of view,
Making, in all, a pretty crew,
To take our town of Orleans.

To *Ile au Chat* their fleet first steer'd,
Where near a hundred sail appear'd;
And, from their numbers, many fear'd
Th' impending fate of Orleans.

They enter'd *Bayou Bienvenu*,
Where there were traitors not a few,
To help them on and bring them thro'
To this our town of Orleans.

They to the *Levee* quickly come,
And made, as tho' they were at home—
Indeed, they were but eight miles from
The very town of Orleans.

The news at last to JACKSON came;
His mighty soul was in a flame,
He swore an oath; I dare not name,
He'd save the town of Orleans.

The town was in a mighty rout;
He order'd all the forces out;
His troops so steady and so stout,
To fight and bleed for Orleans.

Away went JACKSON at their head,
And many a gallant man he led;
All swore they'd fight till they were dead,
To save the town of Orleans.

The *English* camp he's soon among;
And found them near five thousand strong,
From swamp to river stretch'd along
Against the town of Orleans.

And now began a bloody fight;
The *English* heroes tried their might,
But many think the coming night
Did save the town of Orleans.

Then JACKSON, not to risk the town,
Retired for a while his sport down,
And somehow [illegible], and raised a mound,
To save the town of Orleans.

The *English* grown twelve thousand strong,
The [illegible] again come on,
[illegible] would soon belong
To them, as well as Orleans.

[illegible] *New Years* [illegible] came,
[illegible] that day were serv'd the same,
And [illegible] they got no fame
From those who fought for Orleans.

But 'twas the *English* they tried their might,
And brought their [illegible],
And swore that men would at the fight,
All fly towards New Orleans.

That morning's [illegible] in blood;
[illegible] all our men right valiant stood,
As every [illegible] *Yankee* should
Against the foes of Orleans.

The muskets and the cannons roar;
Our men [illegible];
And rolling [illegible] before,
Upon the foes of Orleans.

Sir Edward led the eager crew,
And pointing to the town in view,
Gave them the sack and pillage too,
If they would get to Orleans.

But [illegible],
And *Gibbs* too lies among the dead,
With many more who [illegible] fled,
They'd [illegible] that day at Orleans.

Such carnage ne'er was known before;
More than three thousand stain our shore,
And some [illegible] a thousand more
Of the proud foes of Orleans.

Soldiers! you've had no vulgar game!
Wellington's troops here yield their fame;
INVINCIBLES was once their name,
But this day's [illegible] near Orleans.

A bloodless victory, on our side,
May well increase our general's pride;
For few—the field is only dyed
With *English* blood near Orleans.

The proud, but disappointed foe
Is now [illegible] our worth to know,
And all they ask, is but to go
Far——away from Orleans.

See how their heroes scour the plain!
Their boats can scarce their rage restrain,
So anxious now their fleet to gain,
And get away from Orleans.

Aboard, and sick of *Yankee* sport,
They're drawing up a long report,
To fool their Gracious Sovereign's court,
Of their great [illegible] Orleans.

Here's to the [illegible] a brilliant day!
To pride to have been in the affray,
Which drove the *English* [illegible] away
From this our town of Orleans.

Here's to the gallant GENERAL! who
Has saved our town and country too!
A braver man the world ne'er knew,
Than he who fought for Orleans.

BRAVE SONS OF TENNESSEE! a toast!
Of you, your country well may boast;
She cannot find a braver host
'Mong those who fought for Orleans.

Grand Battle of

N. ORLEANS,

UNDER THE VETERAN

General Andrew Jackson,

The second WASHINGTON of America,

On the memorable 8th of January 1815,

In which Yankee skill & bravery will forever stand on record unparalelled in history.

Chain of our Union indissoluble!

BATTLE OF PATTSBURGH,

AND

VICTORY ON LAKE CHAMPLAIN,

In which 14,000 *British myrmidons* were defeated and put to flight by 5,000 *Yankees* and *Green-mountain Boys*, on the memorable Eleventh of Sept, 1814.

Tune—"Battle of the Kegs."

SIR GEORGE PREVOST with all his host
March'd forth from Montreal, Sir,
Both he and they as blithe and gay
As going to a ball, Sir.
The troops he chose were all of those
That conquer'd Marshal SOULT, Sir,
Who at *Garonne* (the fact is known)
Scarce brought them to a halt, Sir.

With troops like these he tho't with ease
To crush the Yankee faction:
His only thought was how he ought
To bring them into action.
Your very names, Sir GEORGE exclaims,
Without a gun or bay'net,
Will pierce like darts thro' Yankee hearts,
And all their spirits stagnate.

Oh! how I dread, lest they have fled
And left their puny Fort, Sir.
For sure MACOMB won't stay at home,
To afford us any sport, Sir.
Good-bye, he said to those that stay'd,
Keep close as mice, or rats snug,
We just run out upon a scout,
To burn the town of PLATTSBURGH.

Then up *Champlain* with might & main
He march'd with dread array, Sir,
With Fife and Drum to scare MACOMB,
And drive him quite away, Sir.
And side by side their nations pride,
Along the current beat, Sir;
Sworn not to sup 'till they eat up
Macdonough and his fleet, Sir,

Still onward came these men of fame,
[illegible] to give [illegible] quarter;
But to their cost found out at last
That they had caught a tartar,
At distance shot awhile they fought
By water and by land, Sir,
His *Knightship* ran from man to man,
And gave his dread command, Sir.

"*Britons*, strike home, this dog *Macomb*,
So well the fellow knows us—
Will just as soon jump o'er the moon
As venture to oppose us:
With quick dispatch light ev'ry match,
Man ev'ry gun and swivel,
Cross in a crack the *Saranack*,
And drive 'em to the Devil!"

The *Vermont* ranks that lin'd the banks
Then pois'd the unerring rifle,
And to oppose their haughty foes,
They found a perfect trifle.
Meanwhile the fort kept up such sport,
They thought the devil was in it;
Their mighty train play'd off in vain—
'Twas silenc'd in a minute.

Sir GEORGE amaz'd, so wildly gaz'd,
Such frantic gambols acted,
Of all his men not one in ten,
But thought him quite distracted.
He curs'd and swore, his hair he tore,
Then jump'd upon his poney,
And gallop'd off towards the bluff,
To look for Captain Downie.

But when he spy'd M'Donough ride,
In all the pomp of glory,
He hasten'd back to Saranac,
To tell the dismal story;
"My gallant crews, oh shocking news!
Are all or kill'd or taken!
Except a few that just withdrew
In time to save their bacon.

Old England's pride must now subside,
Oh! how the news will shock her,
To have her fleet not only beat,
But sent to Davy's locker!
From this sad day let no one say,
Britannia rules the ocean,
We've dearly bought the humbling tho't
That this is all a notion.

We won't give up the Ship.—We won't give up the Soil.—Free trade, Sailor's rights, and no impressment.

BRITISH LION.

M'DONOUGH'S SHIP.

CAPT. DOWNIE.

GEN. MACOMB.

GOV. PREVOST.

GENIUS OF AMERICA
in Combat with
OLD JONNY BULL.

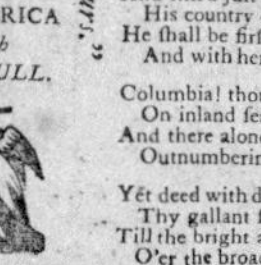

[*COPY-RIGHT* [illegible]]

"Millions for Defence.—Not a Cent for Tribute."—"We have met the enemy, and they are ours."

With one to ten, I'd fight 'gainst MEN,
But these are Satan's legions,
With malice fraught, come piping hot
From Pluto's darkest regions!
Helas, mon Dieu! what shall I do,
I smell the burning sulphur,
Set Britain's isle all rank and file—
Such men would soon engulph her.

That's full as bad, oh! I'll run mad,
Those western hounds are summon'd;
Gaines, Scott & Brown are coming down,
To serve me just like Drummond.
Thick too as bees the Vermontese,
Are swarming on the lake, sir;
And Izard's men come back again,
Lie hid in every brake, sir!

Good Brisbane, beat a quick retreat,
Before their forces join, sir,
For sure as fate they've laid a bait,
To catch us like Burgoyne, sir,
All round about, keep good look out,
We'll surely be surrounded,
Since I could crawl my gallant soul
Was never so astounded."

The rout began, Sir GEORGE led on,
His men ran helter skelter,
Each try'd his best t'out run the rest
To gain a place of shelter;
To hide their fear they gave a cheer,
And thought it mighty cunning—
He'll fight, say they, another day,
Who saves himself by running!

COMMODORE

MACDONOUGH's VICTORY.

O FREEMEN, raise a joyous strain!
Aloft the Eagle towers,
"*We've met the enemy*" again—
Again have made them 'OURS!'

Champlain! the cannon's thundering voice,
Proclaims thy waters free;
Thy forest-waving hills rejoice,
And echo—*Victory!*

The striped flag upon thy wave,
Triumphantly appears,
And to invested landsmen, brave,
A star of promise bears.

Now to the world Fame's trumpet sounds
The deed with new applause,
While from a *Conquer'd Fleet* resounds,
Our seamen's loud huzzas.

Britannia, round thy haggard brows
Bind bitter wormwood still;
For lo! again thy standard bows
To valiant Yankee skill.

But, O! what chaplet can be found
MACDONOUGH's brows to grace?
'Tis done! the glorious wreath is bound,
Which time can ne'er efface,

And still a just—a rich reward,
His country has to give;
He shall be first in her regard,
And with her PERRY live!

Columbia! though thy cannon's roar
On inland seas prevail,
And there alone—while round each shore
Outnumbering ships assail.

Yet deed with deed, and name with name
Thy gallant sons shall blend,
Till the bright arch of naval fame,
O'er the broad ocean bend!

COLUMBIA, represented as surrounded by enemies.

Battle of Niagara!

OR,

AMERICA again victorious over her white and red savage Enemies!

O'ER Huron's wave the sun was low,
The weary soldier watch'd the bow,
Fast fading from the cloud below
The dashing of Niagara.

And while the phantom chain'd his sight
Ah! little thought he of the fight—
The horrors of the dreamless night,
That posted on so rapidly.

Soon, soon as fled each softer charm,
The drum and trumpet sound alarm,
And bid each warrior nerve his arm,
For boldest deeds of chivalry.

The burning red cross, waving high,
Like meteor in the evening sky,
Proclaims the haughty foeman nigh,
To try the strife of rivalry.

Columbia's banner floats as proud,
Her gallant band around it crowd,
And swear to guard or make their shroud
The starred flag of liberty.

"Haste, haste thee, SCOTT, to meet the foe
And let the scornful Briton know,
Well strung the arm and firm the blow
Of him who strikes for liberty."

Loud, loud the din of battle rings,
Shrill through the ranks the bullet sings
And onward fierce each foeman springs
To meet his peer in gallantry.

Behind the hills descends the sun,
The work of death is but begun,
And red through twilight's shadows dun
Blazes the vollied musketry.

"Charge, MILLER, charge the foe once more,"
And louder than Niagara's roar,
Along the line is heard encore,
"On, on to death or victory.

From line to line with lurid glow,
High arching shoots the rocket's bow,
And lights the mingled scene below
Of carnage, death, and misery.

The middle watch has now begun,
The horrid battle fray is done,
Nor longer beats the furious drum,
To death, to death or victory

All, all is still—with silent tread,
The watchman steals among the dead,
To guard his comrade's lowly head,
Till morning give him sepulchre.

Low in the West, of splendor shorn,
The midnight moon with bloody horn,
Sheds her last beam on him forlorn
Who fell in fight so gloriously.

Oh! long her crescent wax and wane,
Ere she behold such fray again,
Such dismal night, such heaps of slain,
Foe mix't with foe promiscuously.

COLUMBIA, finally victorious over all her enemies—reclining in Peace, and surrounded with plenty.

WINDSOR, (Vt.)
Printed for the Flying Book-Sellers,
Jan. 1, 1815.

A British General, surrounded and taken by Yankee light horse.

Lord *Castlereagh*, mounted on a Goat, in the attitude of delivering his late "*Sine qua non*" to the British ministers at Ghent.

British Colonel in a fright,
Lost his hat in the fight,
Running off in the night,
What a laughable fight!

Lieutenant-Col. Barnes,
To keep up shins and sides,
Upon a Camel mounts
And off in shame he rides!

The valiant Major Bright,
Astride the Goose perforce,
And hastes to Montreal,
To tell the horrid news!

The Indian Chief so bent on prey,
Of Infant scalping who can tell
The horrors of that dismal day,
Where echo groans with savage yell?

A Vermonter, attacking the veterans of Lord Wellington, while crossing the fatal river.

A British chief from horse doth fall,
Brought down by force of Yankee Ball.

The God of War *mows down the enemy by hundreds, and crimsons the waters of the Saranac with blood!*

In 30 minutes, said the British Commodore, I will be on board Macdonough's ship; but behold him slain the first fire, and his ship a wreck!

A few British Gun Boats barely escape to carry the dismal tidings of defeat and destruction of their Fleet.

With pain and wo,
Death strikes the foe
A heavy blow,
And lays him low.

Gov. Gen. of the Canadas arrested for cowardice, and seated on an Elephant.

NUMBER 12

NEWS of the peace signed at Ghent on Christmas Eve, 1814, could never have reached Louisiana in time to restrain British and American armies from fighting the two-week long Battle of New Orleans. In the main battle on January 8, 1815, 2,000 British and West Indian troops of General Edward Pakenham were killed or wounded. Pakenham himself and two of his generals were among the dead. Only thirteen of Andrew Jackson's 3,500 regulars and militia were killed in the battle that, as Admiral Morison has said, ended "the 'Second War of Independence' in a blaze of glory," dimmed American memories of previous defeats, and paved the way for Andrew Jackson to enter the White House in 1828 after gaining the popular vote in 1824 but losing the election in the House of Representatives.

DATE: 1816

LOCATION: American Antiquarian Society

SIZE: 60 x 50 cm.

Politics & Statecraft

IN CONGRESS,

MAY 15, 1776.

WHEREAS his Britannic Majesty, in conjunction with the Lords and Commons of Great-Britain, has by a late Act of Parliament excluded the inhabitants of these United Colonies from the protection of his Crown: AND WHEREAS no answer whatever to the humble Petitions of the Colonies for redress of grievances and reconciliation with Great-Britain, has been or is likely to be given; but the whole force of that kingdom, aided by foreign mercenaries, is to be exerted for the destruction of the good people of these Colonies: AND WHEREAS it appears absolutely irreconcileable to reason and good conscience, for the people of these Colonies now to take the oaths and affirmations necessary for the support of any government under the Crown of Great-Britain, and it is necessary that the exercise of every kind of authority under the said Crown should be totally suppressed, and all the powers of government exerted under the people of the Colonies, for the preservation of internal peace, virtue and good order, as well as for the defence of their lives, liberties and properties against the hostile invasions and cruel depredations of their enemies:—

RESOLVED therefore, That it be recommended to the respective Assemblies and Conventions of the United Colonies, where no government sufficient to the exigencies of their affairs has been hitherto established, to adopt such government as shall in the opinion of the Representatives of the people best conduce to the happiness and safety of their constituents in particular and America in general.

Extract from the Minutes,

CHARLES THOMSON, Secretary.

To the INHABITANTS *of* VERMONT, *a Free and Independent* State, *bounding on the River* CONNECTICUT *and Lake* CHAMPLAIN.

GENTLEMEN, PHILADELPHIA, April 11, 1777.

NUMBERS of you are knowing to the zeal with which I have exerted myself in your behalf from the beginning of your struggle with the New-York Monopolizers. As the Supreme Arbiter of right has smiled on the just cause of North-America at large, you in a peculiar manner have been highly favored. God has done by you the best thing commonly done for our species. He has put it fairly in your power to help yourselves.

I have taken the minds of several leading Members in the Honorable the Continental Congress, and can assure you that you have nothing to do but send attested copies of the Recommendation to take up government to every township in your district, and invite all your freeholders and inhabitants to meet in their respective townships and chuse members for a General Convention, to meet at an early day to chuse Delegates for the General Congress, a Committee of Safety, and to form a Constitution for your State.

Your friends here tell me that some are in doubt whether Delegates from your district would be admitted into Congress. I tell you to organize fairly, and make the experiment, and I will ensure your success at the risque of my reputation as a man of honor or common sense. Indeed they can by no means refuse you! You have as good a right to chuse how you will be governed, and by whom, as they had.

I have recommended to your Committee the Constitution of Pennsylvania for a model, which, with a very little alteration, will, in my opinion, come as near perfection as any thing yet concerted by mankind. This Constitution has been sifted with all the criticism that a band of despots were masters of, and has bid defiance to their united powers.

The alteration I would recommend is, that all the Bills intended to be passed into Laws should be laid before the Executive Board for their perusal and proposals of amendment. All the difference then between such a Constitution and those of Connecticut and Rhode-Island, in the grand outlines is, that in one case the Executive power can advise and in the other compel. For my own part, I esteem the people at large the true proprietors of governmental power. They are the supreme constituent power, and of course their immediate Representatives are the supreme delegate power; and as soon as the delegate power gets too far out of the hands of the constituent power, a tyranny is in some degree established.

Happy are you that in laying the foundation of a new government, you have a digest drawn from the purest fountains of antiquity, and improved by the readings and observations of the great Doctor FRANKLIN, DAVID RITTENHOUSE, Esq; and others. I am certain you may build on such a basis a system which will transmit liberty and happiness to posterity.

Let the scandalous practice of bribing men by places, commissions, &c. be held in abhorrence among you. By entrusting only men of capacity and integrity in public affairs, and by obliging even the best men to fall into the common mass of the people every year, and be sensible of their need of the popular good will to sustain their political importance, is your liberties well secured. These plans effectually promise this security.

May Almighty God smile upon your arduous and important undertaking, and inspire you with that wisdom, virtue, public spirit and unanimity, which ensures success in the most hazardous enterprizes!

I am, Gentlemen, Your sincere friend and humble servant,

THOMAS YOUNG.

APRIL 12, 1777.

YOUR Committee have obtained for you a copy of the Recommendation of Congress to all such bodies of men as looked upon themselves returned to a state of nature, to adopt such government as should in the opinion of the Representatives of the people best conduce to the happiness and safety of their constituents in particular and America in general.

You may perhaps think strange that nothing further is done for you at this time than to send you this extract. But if you consider that till you incorporate and actually announce to Congress your having become a body politic, they cannot treat with you as a free State. While New-York claims you as subjects of that government, my humble opinion is, your own good sense will suggest to you, that no time is to be lost in availing yourselves of the same opportunity your assuming mistress is improving to establish a dominion for herself and you too.

A WORD TO THE WISE IS SUFFICIENT.

A convention of delegates from various towns in Vermont gathered at Westminster, January 15, 1777, and declared that the area of the New Hampshire Grants "ought to be and is forever hereafter a free and independent jurisdiction and state." When the Continental Congress sitting in Philadelphia refused to recognize the independence of the Grants, Ira Allen published a pamphlet claiming the rights of independence, which Dr. Thomas Young, intellectual mentor of Ira's brother Ethan, supported in a series of letters to both the Congress and to residents of the newly proclaimed independent Grants.

Young, according to Ira Allen's *History of Vermont*, had his call for an election of delegates printed as a broadside in Philadelphia, distributed it widely through the Grants, and thus persuaded the drafters of Vermont's Constitution to model their document on that of Pennsylvania. The actual author of the Constitution is unknown, though both Young and Ira Allen have been credited with its composition. The Constitution of Vermont was read and adopted at Windsor in July 1777, in the midst of a vigorous thunderstorm and under threat of the British army of General Burgoyne encamped at Crown Point less than seventy miles to the west across the range of Green Mountains.

DATE: 1777

LOCATION: John Carter Brown Library
Brown University

SIZE: 31.5 x 24.5 cm.

BY HIS EXCELLENCY

THOMAS CHITTTENDEN, Esq;

Governor and Commander in Chief in and over the State of *VERMONT*, in AMERICA,

A PROCLAMATION.

AMID the many private and public Distresses of a temporal Nature, Arguments for Praise and Thanksgiving multiply and arise from almost every Quarter;---as it is of the LORD'S *Mercies that we are not consumed, and because his Compassions fail not:----But the many Favors and Blessings, in particular, with which we, as a People, have been indulged in the Course of the past Year, lay us under renewed Obligations to ascribe a Tribute of Praise and Thanksgiving to Almighty* GOD, *the beneficent Author of all Good.*

I HAVE therefore thought fit, by and with the Advice of the Council, and at the Desire of the Representatives of the Freemen of this State, in General Assembly met,—to appoint, and do hereby appoint THURSDAY the TWENTY-SIXTH DAY OF NOVEMBER next, to be observed as a Day of public THANKSGIVING throughout this State;—exhorting all Denominations and Orders of People; to present their Thank-Offering at the Throne of Grace, and pay their Vows to the LORD;—to praise his holy Name for all the Bounties of his Providence, and the far richer Blessings of his Grace, in which we share:——Especially to ascribe Honor, Praise, and Thanksgiving to our GOD for the Enjoyment of the inestimable Privileges of the Gospel:—For that Unanimity, which subsists in the public Councils of the United States:—For the Readiness of the People to stand forth in the Defence of their invaluable Rights and Liberties:—For divine Interposition in raising up a powerful Ally in Favor of the United States:—For every Instance of Protection and Success granted us and our Allies, both by Sea and Land, against our potent and inveterate Foes:—For that Measure of Health enjoyed in the Country and Army:—For a competent Supply of the former and latter Harvest;—And for every Expression of his loving Kindness and tender Mercy.——And at the same Time, to implore GOD'S gracious Presence with the GENERAL CONGRESS of the United States of America;—That he would give them Wisdom, Ability and Fidelity equal to their important Trust;—That all our Assemblies and Councils may be owned and blessed:—That he would continue the Life of our Commander in Chief, and afford him divine Guidance and Direction:—That he would form our Generals, Officers and Soldiery for their respective Departments, and, yet further, honor them as Instruments of our Deliverance:—That he would pour out his Spirit, in plentiful Effusions, on Ministers and People of all Denominations, in this and all the States:—That Seminaries of Learning and Schools of Instruction may be, every where among us, promoted and succeeded:—That the People of this State, in particular, may be blessed in all their spiritual and temporal Concerns:—That they may be enabled to adopt such Measures, and pursue such Plans, as may most effectually tend to Peace, Unanimity and good Order:—That GOD would yet make us glad, according to the Days wherein we have been afflicted, and the Time in which we have seen Evil:—That he would look down in Pity and tender Compassion on this State, in its Infancy; delight to own and bless it; and grant it may find Favor in the Sight of the grand Council of AMERICA:—That this once howling Wilderness may, in a spiritual Sense, bud and blossom like the Rose:—That he will be pleased to bless and prosper the Work of our Hands;—Establish his Covenant with us and our Children to the latest Posterity:—And fill the Universe with a Display of his glorious Perfections, through our Lord and Saviour JESUS CHRIST.

All servile Labour is forbidden on said Day.

Given under my Hand in Council, at Windsor, this 18th Day of October, in the Year of our Lord 1778.

THOS. CHITTENDEN.

By His Excellency's Command,

Matthew Lyon, Sec'ry Pro. Tem.

NUMBER 14

ON March 30, 1778, President Eleazar Wheelock of Dartmouth College began efforts to bring a printer to the northern Connecticut River Valley in the New Hampshire Grants. He tried to arrange first for Timothy Green of Norwich, Connecticut, who had been official New Haven Colony printer since 1763, to bring his business north. Finally toward the end of August 1778, Green sent Alden Spooner with a press and other printing materials to Dresden, now Hanover, New Hampshire. The products of Spooner's press, known as Dresden Imprints, survive today in the form of nearly fifty books and broadsides. One of the earliest is the broadside calling for the observance of Thanksgiving in Vermont by Governor Thomas Chittenden on October 18, 1778.

DATE: 1778

LOCATION: Dartmouth College

SIZE: 41.5 x 33 cm.

STATE OF VERMONT.

In COUNCIL, Windſor, 7th June, 1779.

RESOLVED, *That the Captain-General's orders of the 6th of May laſt, to Colonel Ethan Allen, together with an extract of the proceedings of the adjourned Superior Court, held at Weſtminſter, in the ſouth Halfſhire of the county of Cumberland, on the 26th day of May laſt, and his Excellency's proclamation of the 3d inſtant, be publiſhed.*

Extract from the minutes, JONAS FAY, *Secretary pro temp.*

ORDERS to Colonel *Ethan Allen*, &c.

WHEREAS complaint hath been made unto me by Samuel Fletcher, Eſq; commanding the firſt regiment of militia within this ſtate, that on Wedneſday, the 28th day of April laſt, at Putney, in the ſtate aforeſaid, a large number of men, conſiſting of near one hundred, being unlawfully aſſembled under the command of a certain pretended Colonel Pattiſon, of Hinſdale, did then and there, by force and with violence take and convey from one William M'Waine, a ſerjeant belonging to Captain Daniel Jewet's company of militia, and in the ſaid Samuel Fletcher's regiment, two cows, which the ſaid Serjeant M'Waine had previouſly taken one from James Clay and the other from Benjamin Willſon, both of Putney, by virtue of a warrant by legal authority, directing the ſaid Serjeant M'Waine to diſpoſe of ſo much of the eſtates of the ſaid James Clay and Benjamin Willſon, at public outcry, as would ſatisfy the fines of the ſaid James and Benjamin's refuſing to march, or pay their proportion of raiſing men when legally drafted for the ſervice of this and the United States of America, agreeable to an act of the General Aſſembly of the repreſentatives of the freemen of this ſtate; and praying for relief in the premiſes, as being againſt the peace and dignity of the ſame:

You are therefore hereby commanded, in the name of the freemen of the ſtate of Vermont, to engage one hundred able bodied effective men, as volunteers in the county of Bennington, and to march them into the county of Cumberland, ſeaſonably to aſſiſt the Sheriff of ſaid county to execute ſuch orders as he has, or may receive from the civil authority of this ſtate, in order to put into execution at the adjourned ſeſſions of the Superior Court, to be holden at Weſtminſter, in the county aforeſaid, the 26th day of May inſtant. Hereof you may not fail. Given under my hand, at Arlington, this 6th day of May, A. D. 1779.

THOMAS CHITTENDEN, Captain-General.

State of Vermont. } *At an adjourned Superior Court holden at Weſtminſter, in the county of Cumberland, on the 26th of May, 1779.*

PRESENT.

MOSES ROBINSON, Eſquire, Chief Judge.
JOHN SHEPHERDSON, Eſq;
JOHN FASSET, jun. Eſq;
THOMAS CHANDLER, jun. Eſq; and
JOHN THROOP, Eſq;
} Side Judges of the ſame.

Noah Smith, State-Attorney within and for ſaid county, exhibited complaint, that

Eleazar Patterſon, of Hinſdale, in ſaid county; Elkanah Day, Michael Gilſon, Benjamin Whitney, Medad Wright, Bela Willard, Joſeph Willard, Beldad Eaſton, John Norton and John Seſſions, each of Weſtminſter, in ſaid county.

Michael Townſhend, John Serjeants, Timothy Church, James Blakeſlee, Samuel Root and Benjamin Butterfield, each of Brattleborough, in ſaid county; and James Clay, Lucas Willſon, James Clay, jun. Ephraim Clay, Daniel Saben, Noah Saben, William Pierce, Noah Cuſhion, Samuel Wheat, Francis Cummings, James Cummings, Thomas Pierce, Joſeph Joy and Thomas Nelſon, each of Putney, in ſaid county, did on or about the 28th day of April laſt paſt, at Putney aforeſaid, in a riotous and unlawful manner, by force and arms, an aſſault make upon one William M'Waine, then a lawful officer in the execution of a lawful command, and did alſo then and there, viz. with force aforeſaid, apprehend and reſcue out of the hands and poſſeſſion of the ſaid M'Waine two cows, which the ſaid M'Waine had taken by lawful command from lawful authority, which wicked conduct was a flagrant violation of the common law of the land, and contrary to the force and effect of a certain ſtatute law of this ſtate, entituled, "An Act "to prevent Riots, Diſorders and Contempt of Authority "within this State, and for puniſhing the ſame," as per complaint on file, dated the 26th day of May, 1779.

The delinquents aforeſaid being brought into Court, and put to plead to ſaid information: Plead in bar to that part of the ſaid information grounded on the ſtatute in the following words, viz.

"That although by common law they might be holden to anſwer the information, yet they could not be holden to anſwer that part thereof brought on the ſtatute, and that becauſe 'twas not in the power of the perſons complained of to have known that ſtatute at the time when the crimes were ſaid to have been committed, the ſaid ſtatute not having been promulgated; and this they were ready to verify.

Judgment, &c. &c.

BRADLEY, for delinquents."

The Court overruled the abovesaid plea in bar to be ſufficient, and ordered that part of the information brought on the ſtatute to be diſmiſſed.

The delinquents then plead to General Iſſue, Not guilty, and gave in evidence, that they were ſubjects of the ſtate of N. York, and the facts charged againſt them in the aforeſaid information, were done by virtue of authority granted them by the ſtate of N. York, and thereof put themſelves upon the Court for trial.------Judgment, &c. &c.

The Court having heard the evidence, and fully conſidered the cauſe, gave judgment, that the delinquents complained of as aforeſaid were guilty, and that

Eleazar Patterſon, John Serjeants, Elkanah Day and James Clay aforeſaid pay a fine, each of Forty pounds lawful money, to the Treaſurer of this ſtate.

That Michael Gilſon, Lewis Willſon and Timothy Church aforeſaid pay a fine, each of Twenty-five pounds lawful money, to the Treaſurer of this ſtate.

That Micah Townſhend, James Blakeſlee, James Clay, jun. Benjamin Whitney, Samuel Root, John Norton and John Seſſions aforeſaid, pay a fine, each of Twenty pounds lawful money, to the Treaſurer of this ſtate.

That Ephraim Clay, Medad Wright, Bela Willard, Joſeph Willard and Bildad Eaſton aforeſaid pay a fine, each of Ten pounds lawful money, to the Treaſurer of this ſtate.

That Daniel Sabin, Noah Sabin, William Pierce, Noah Cuſhion, Samuel Wheat, Francis Cummings, James Cummings, Joſeph Joy, Thomas Pierce and Thomas Willſon aforeſaid pay a fine, each of Three pounds lawful money, to the Treaſurer of this ſtate; and that Benjamin Butterfield aforeſaid pay a fine, of Forty ſhillings lawful money, to the Treaſurer of this ſtate.----And that the delinquents aforeſaid pay coſt of proſecution, taxed at £1477 : 18 : 0.

A true extract from the original records.
Examined and atteſted by
STEPHEN R. BRADLEY, *Clerk pro temp.*

By his Excellency THOMAS CHITTENDEN, *Eſquire, Governor, Captain-General, and Commander in Chief, in and over the State of* Vermont,

A PROCLAMATION.

Seal.

WHEREAS ſundry perſons, inhabitants of this ſtate, forgetting that great tie of allegiance that ought to bind every ſubject in a faithful obedience to that power which protects life, liberty and fortune. Being inſtigated partly through their own miſtaken notions of government, not conſidering all power originates from the people, and building on a falſe reaſon, that a public acknowledgment of the powers of the earth is eſſential to the exiſtence of a diſtinct ſeparate ſtate, but more eſpecially being deceived and influenced by certain perſons who have crept in privily to ſpy out and overturn the liberties of this ſtate, purchaſed at the deareſt rate, who acting under pretence of power aſſumed by a neighbouring ſiſter ſtate, never derived from God or nature, have impoſed their tenets on the credulous, whereby ſome have been led to follow their pernicious ways, in conſequence of which ſome of my faithful ſubjects have been traduced to oppoſe the authority of this ſtate, and obſtruct the courſe of civil law, to the diſturbance of the peace, thereby incurring the penalties of that great rule of right which requires obedience to the powers that are.

And whereas the ſupreme authority of this ſtate are ever willing to alleviate the miſeries of thoſe unhappy ſubjects who tranſgreſs laws through miſtaken notions, in remitting the penalties thereof, and in as much as equal puniſhments (in this caſe) cannot be diſtributed without puniſhing the righteous with the wicked:

I have therefore thought fit, by and with the advice of Council, and at the deſire of the repreſentatives of the freemen of this ſtate, in General Aſſembly met, to make known and declare this my gracious deſign of mercy to every offender, and do hereby publiſh and declare to all perſons reſiding within this ſtate, a full and free pardon of all public offences, crimes and miſdemeanors heretofore committed within the limits of the ſame, againſt the honour and dignity of the freemen thereof, remitting to all and ſingular the perſons aforeſaid, all penalties incurred for breaches of the peace, ſuch as riots, mobs, tumultuous aſſemblies, contempt of and oppoſition to authority, excepting only the crimes of high treaſon, miſpriſion of treaſon, and other capital offences committed ſince the 15th day of January, 1777, and all perſons indicted, informed againſt, or complained of for any of the offences aforeſaid, committed before this date, may plead this proclamation in diſcharge thereof, provided nothing herein contained be conſtrued to extend to any perſon againſt whom judgment has been already rendered, nor to bar any perſon from recovering private damages, any thing contained herein to the contrary notwithſtanding.

And I do further aſſure the ſubjects of this ſtate, that it is not the deſign of government to take from any one the peaceable enjoyment of his own poſſeſſions acquired by the ſweat of his brow, whatever falſhoods wicked and deſigning men may have invented to diſquiet the minds of the faithful ſubjects of the ſtate of Vermont.

Given under my hand and ſeal at arms, in the Council Chamber, at Windſor, on the 3d day of June, 1779, in the third year of the independence of this and the United States of America.

THOMAS CHITTENDEN.

By his Excellency's command,
JONAS FAY, *Secretary pro temp.*

GOD SAVE THE PEOPLE!

NUMBER 15

ALTHOUGH the main action of the Revolutionary War had passed to the South after the Battle of Saratoga, the late 1770's remained troubled years for the infant state of Vermont. In 1779, with Independence only two years old, New York still claimed legal authority over lands on both sides of the Green Mountains range. Governor Thomas Chittenden and his Council had a light grip on the reins of Vermont's young government. Cumberland County in eastern Vermont presented some especially difficult problems of jurisdiction and authority. A number of the land grants there had been made by the provincial governor of colonial New York before the Revolution, and the owners of those lands after Independence refused to recognize the authority of Chittenden's government in the region of Putney and Brattleboro.

Tensions grew when James Clay and Benjamin Willson, having refused to answer the Governor's muster call or pay for a substitute, were fined two cows, and the animals were then confiscated by William M'Ilwaine, a sergeant of militia. Nearly one hundred men of the Putney region, including some like Micah Townsend who would eventually migrate to Canada as a Loyalist, took the cows away from Sergeant M'Ilwaine, thereby apparently leaving Chittenden only one course —to order Ethan Allen and his men from Bennington to assist Chittenden's Cumberland County sheriff in the execution of the Government's orders in early May 1779.

Later in May the Superior Court of Cumberland County found thirty-one of the resisting New York-granted landholders guilty of assaulting Sergeant M'Ilwaine "in a riotous and unlawful manner" and thus in violation of the common and statutory laws of Vermont.

But Thomas Chittenden was a wise and clever politician. By proclamation on June 3 he pardoned the thirty-one Cumberland rioters and forgave them the fines and fees of nearly £2,000, including in his pardon all other public offenders guilty of violations since January 15. By circulating the major legal documents surrounding the Cumberland Riots, especially the General Pardon, as printed by Alden Spooner, Chittenden hoped to unify and gain further support for the newly independent state of Vermont.

DATE: 1779

LOCATION: Library Company of Philadelphia

SIZE: 44.5 x 33 cm.

TO THE PEOPLE OF VERMONT.

FELLOW CITIZENS,

IT IS DONE! The cup of guilt is full! Treaſon, rebellion and murder ſtalk abroad at noon-day! Our land has been ſtained with the blood of our citizens, acting in defence of the government and laws of our country. By whom? A foreign foe? No: but, (horrid to relate!) by the bloody hands of domeſtic traitors.

Capt. JONATHAN ORMSBY, a reſpectable farmer, belonging to Burlington; Mr. ELLIS DRAKE and Mr. ASA MARSH, two reſpectable young men, belonging to Capt. Pratt's company of militia, ſtationed at Windmill Point, were all killed at Burlington, on Wedneſday the 3d inſtant, about noon, in a moſt wanton and barbarous manner, by a party of inſurgents, employed in ſmuggling potaſh into Canada, in violation of the laws. The Collector detached Lieut. Farrington, a ſergeant and twelve men, in purſuit of a boat, which had gone up Onion river after a load of potaſh.—The Lieutenant found the boat and took poſſeſſion of her, notwithſtanding the inſurgents threatened to blow out his brains if he attempted to meddle with her. The Lieutenant dropped down the river, with the cutter and the boat he had taken, about half a mile; when the inſurgents fired upon him and killed Drake. The Lieutenant then ordered both boats to be rowed on ſhore, near the place whence the fire proceeded: he landed with his men, and aſcended the bank of the river;—immediately the inſurgents diſcharged a large gun, called a wall-piece, the barrel of which is eight feet in length, and was loaded with ſixteen ounce balls, and ſome buck ſhot—which carried inſtant death to Captain Ormſby and Mr. Marſh, ſeverely wounded the Lieutenant in the head, the left arm, and ſlightly wounded him in the right ſhoulder. Capt. Ormſby had been laboring in his field during the forenoon, near the fatal ſpot, was on his return to dinner, had juſt reached the place where the government troops entered the road, when the murderous diſcharge took place, which, at the ſame inſtant, ſent two ſouls companions into eternity.

If any thing can add to the horror of this, too horrid ſcene, it is the obſervation of certain federal characters of the vicinity, who even lay claim to the name of high reſpectability, tending to ſcreen the aſſaſſins, and throw the whole weight of guilt on the part of the government.——Says one, *The men were ſent here by Penniman to ſteal an empty boat, and died like fools*—Says another, *I hope to God Penniman will be hung for it*—Says another, *I ſhould care but little about it, if I did not fear it would influence the enſuing election*—Says another, on hearing of the melancholy event, *I am glad of it, if they are republicans who are killed.*———Such was the current of expreſſion which poured from the mouths of federaliſm, while the blood was ſtill guſhing from the weltering bodies of our countrymen, murdered by federal hands at mid-day, within the boundaries of that town which boaſts itſelf of being the ſtrong hold of federaliſm, and ſome of whoſe principal merchants furniſhed the inſurgents with powder and ball, for the expreſs purpoſe of performing this bloody work.

The federaliſts now begin to lengthen their faces, and pretend to feel regret for the tranſaction; but their hypocritical tears will not avail them. This horrid deed has been done by their procurement; they are partners in the guilt of the perpetrators, and they are accountable to their country and their God, for all the blood that has been ſhed.

When a large body of men, and more eſpecially thoſe in the higher walks of life, who arrogate to themſelves all the virtue, all the talents, and all the religion of the country, combine together for the purpoſe of oppoſing the laws of their country; when they openly and publicly, by printing and ſpeaking, treat the government and the officers of the government, from the Preſident of the United States down to the loweſt executive officer, with abuſe, ridicule and contempt; when they trample on the laws of their country, by daily exciting, both by precept and example, the violation of thoſe laws by force and arms; when they exult at the ſucceſs of the inſurgents in every act of treaſon they commit; when they bid defiance to government, and threaten the officers with aſſaſſination if they attempt to do their duty; when with more than ſavage barbarity they exult over the bleeding bodies of our murdered citizens; and when they even inſult the faithful ſoldier while oppreſſed with grief at the loſs of his beloved comrades:—then is the cup of guilt full; then is it time TO ROUSE IN DEFENCE OF YOUR COUNTRY AND YOUR LIVES.

This is no ordinary conteſt. It is not a ſimple queſtion, who ſhall be governor and councillors; but it is a ſtruggle for the exiſtence of your government; for the protection of thoſe rights purchaſed with the blood of your fathers; and for the protection of your lives. Should that faction whoſe hands are ſtill reeking with the blood of your brethren, come into power, what have you to expect? If they have done theſe things in the face of law, in the face of authority, what will they do when clothed with power? This bloody ſcene is but an opening wedge to the meaſures they would purſue. The tragedy of Roberſpierre would be reacted in the United States; and every diſtinguiſhed character, who is a friend to his country, might expect to be ſacrificed to the malice of an unprincipled and vindictive faction.

Fellow citizens, on you depends the fate of your country—by your ſuffrages at the approaching election, you will decide, whether you deſerve the name of freemen; whether you are worthy of your fathers; whether you will defend the government of your country, and protect your wives, your children, and your own lives; or whether you will tamely give up your dear bought rights, and ſubmit your necks to the axe of the guilotine.

By ſupporting our preſent patriotic governor and councillors, you will perpetuate the exiſtence of our government, and tranſmit to poſterity the bleſſings we now enjoy.

By neglecting to attend the poll, or by voting for the federal ticket, you will entail on your country all the horrors of ſlavery, oppreſſion and murder.

MONITOR.

NUMBER 16

RESISTANCE to the Embargo Act in 1808–09 was strong in northern Vermont. Smuggling of goods and produce, especially lumber and potash on Lake Champlain, was carried on extensively between Vermont and Canada. The *Blacksnake*, a forty-foot single-masted cutter, was one of the most notorious and successful smugglers' ships on the lake in 1808. In this year its crew attempted to prevent federal and militia officers from impounding the boat as it lay beached upstream from the lake on the Winooski River while preparing to receive a new load of potash to carry in to Canada.

A small force of twelve officers and privates surprised the crew of the *Blacksnake* (so-called for its tarred hull) on August 4, 1808. The smugglers, ten of them led by Truman Mudgett of Highgate, resisted and fired on the militiamen as they attempted to sail their customs cutter and the captured *Blacksnake* down the river. Three men were killed by Mudgett's crew. Most of the smugglers were captured at the site of the incident, however, and the remaining fugitives subsequently arrested on or near the border.

The smugglers' trial stirred partisan feelings between Embargo-supporting Republicans and anti-Jefferson Federalists in Vermont. Firmly convinced Federalists, like Ethan Allen, Jr., when called to jury duty, were repeatedly dismissed for holding the opinion that smugglers were innocent of any crime, even murder in this case.

After the Supreme Court of Vermont sat as a grand jury, Royall Tyler presiding chief justice, an indictment was handed down and convictions obtained against most of the crew of the *Blacksnake*. Of the ten smugglers, Cyrus Dean was sentenced to be hanged; the execution was carried out before 10,000 spectators in Burlington on November 11, 1809. Mudgett, however, was finally discharged in 1810 after a *nolle prosequi* was entered in his case. Others who were convicted received sentences that included one hour in the pillory, fifty lashes, and the distinction of being the first convicts incarcerated at Windsor State Prison after its opening in June 1809.

DATE: 1808

LOCATION: Vermont Historical Society

SIZE: 27 x 25 cm.

A Review of New England Politics,

In two Letters from a Clergyman.

DEAR SIR—

THE following communication has rested on my mind for years. Between a consciousness of the effect it would have on me personally, by reason of the great clerical influence in this part of the country, with whom I stood connected, and my sense of duty to the community, I have till now refrained from speaking of it, except to some of my friends. The design of the Congressional clergy have become so alarming to the freedom of religious enquiry, and the liberties of our country, (for they are intimately connected,) I cannot feel excused any longer to remain in silence.

In the year 1799, if my memory serves me right, I heard much said about Mr. Jefferson's infidelity. Wishing to know the certainty of it I called on an acquaintance of mine, who was a member of Congress and told him my business. He gave as I believe, a very candid and correct answer. He considered Mr. Jefferson as the greatest literary character in America, and a man of unblemished morals in his walk in private life. But he attempted to show the importance of having a President from the eastern states, who would consult our interests and defend our rights.

After he had closed these observations, he addressed himself to me in sentiments like these, as near as I can recollect; "I am surprized you have joined that party; you are acting against your own interest. It is understood among the federal party, if they should succeed so far as to have a decided majority in the states, the clergy are to be remembered. We have conversed on the subject, but have not as yet determined, whether it would be best to have them draw their salaries from the public chest at the head of government, or provision made for them to draw from a deposit from each state. This however will be fixed in season. You will then be able to support some dignity of character. You will not then be troubled with the whims and complaints of many in your parish. This is generally understood among the clergy." I replied, that I was afraid of such an establishment: that the persecuting scenes of past ages wo[illegible] return. He observed that we were too enlightened.

[illegible] the time I have observed the conduct of the clergy, and could readily understand their motives. I could clearly understand, Dr. Emmons in his history of Jerusalem, and Dr. Morse in his eulogy over the French priests, who were said to be destroyed, [illegible] whose sentiments and persons the doctor could have no fellowsh[illegible]. The prophetic fate of bibles and meeting houses, depending o[illegible]e issue of the next presidential election, sprang from the same [illegible] This led the clergy to enter into a closer connexion. Where t[illegible] were no state conventions founded, they were immediately attended to. Those conventions meet once a year in each of the states east of the Deleware, and each convention chooses two delegates to represent them in each of the states. They have formed a creed which they have mutually pledged themselves to support. They have concerted their magazines, their missionary labours, their tract societies, and Bible societies, to establish this creed in the minds of the serious part of community. They have established a theological College in Mass. devoted to the same object. They have gone so far in this state, and as far as I know, it is the same in other states as to choose a standing committee to grant a license or liberty to clergymen who come into this state to preach to their churches. They have agreed to have no fellowship with a clergyman who will not procure such a license, and have warned the churches against hearing any one however well he may come recommended, unless he produces such a licence. They have exhorted their churches to excommunicate as heretics all those who will not consent to their creed, insomuch there are in a large portion of the towns among us, those who are excommunicated on this principle. Thus, it appears, the clergy have gotten their national creed prepared before the federal party were ready to receive it.

It is the devotion of my heart, that this design, like the hypocrite's hope, will eventually prove nothing more than a spider's web. Though I am one of those victims whom their policy has given over to feel the effect of their anathema, I still entertain a hope that the civil policy of our common country will never compel me to apply to a creed maker to manufacture a set of articles of faith between me and my Redeemer.

IGNATIUS THOMSON.

DEAR SIR—I feel it a duty to communicate to the public, through the medium of the Herald, a subject which is of some interest to the friends of civil and religious freedom.

In the spring of the year 1807 or 1808, I attended an association of the Congregational clergy at Thetford in this state. After the members had generally convened, a Mr. Fuller, minister of Vershire, observed to Dr. Burton—"Well; you did not succeed in getting Mr. Fowler in a member of the corporation at Burlington." (This college is patronized by the state, and is known by the name of the University of Vermont.) "No," replied the doctor.—"Well what must be done next,' said Mr. Fuller. The doctor affected to be at a loss for an answer. Mr. Worcester, another member of the corporation, replied with some feeling. 'We must withdraw our support from that College, and turn it to Middlebury," (another college in that state under the patronage of individuals.) The doctor then began—"We must turn our influence to Middlebury, and I think we can easily run down the university. When the corporation are convinced, that they cannot support the reputation of the College without the Calvinistic influence, they will be willing to give up Dr. Sanders, (the President) then we can manage that College as we please. It will be of great importance to have it under the Calvinistic influence. To do this, we must cry down the college and Dr. Sanders. We must make the people believe that the reason why the college does not flourish, is because Dr. Sanders is so unpopular. The Calvinistic sentiments never will prevail till the colleges are under our influence. Young men when they go to college generally have not formed their religious sentiments. We ought to have a president and instructors who have the address to instil the Calvinistic sentiments, without the students being sensible of it. Then nine out of ten, when they leave the college will support the Calvinistic doctrines. They will go out in the world, and will have their influence in society. In this way we can get a better support without any law than we have ever had with. And besides, when once all our colleges are under our influence, it will establish our sentiments and influence, so that we can manage the civil government as we please." He then began to name the colleges, and found them all under the calvinistical influence this side of the Delware, (a river peculiarly distinguished in certain men's calculations) "except Brown university, Harvard University, and the University of Vermont. Brown University may be considered as much for us as against us. We have a Divinity College at Andover, which has a great influence over Harvard College, and we think it will soon bring it over to our interest; and we must exert ourselves to obtain this." These are the sentiments, and as nearly the words as I can recollect.

My anxiety to have an understanding with the clergy of the vicinity led me to keep this to myself; but some of them had taken such a decided part against me, that they could not go back without feeling a little mortified; and they concluded it would be better to sacrifice me than to lose them, especially as they considered me a heretic both by their civil and religious creeds.

In the year 1809, I was chosen a member of the general assembly of this state. I then felt it a duty to prevent the designs of the clergy, if possible. Accordingly I brought in a bill to amend the act of establishing the University of Vermont at Burlington. The principal object was to take the right of filling vacancies in the co-operation into the hands of the legislature by a joint ballot of both houses This I considered would always make the College popular, notwithstanding clerical designs. The cry of an unpopular president has been continually sounded; and from some unexpected movement, a majority of the corporation have so far been charmed with the clerical song of an unpopular president, that they have proposed to meet at Montpelier during the session of the legislature, and take into consideration the expediency of removing Dr. Sanders from the presidency. The corporation will then be altogether, and I trust the mojority will not be duped by such designs.

I understand the malcontents have their eye fixed on a Dr. Blanchford, of Lansingburgh, N. Y. as one who is capable of instilling Calvinistic sentiments, without the students being sensible of it.

The heart is deceitful above all things, and desparately wicked; who can know it? IGNATIUS THOMSON.

POMFRET, Sept. 27, 1813.

NUMBER 17

ALTHOUGH Ignatius Thomson (1774–1848) ministered to the Pomfret Congregational Church, his politics were, unlike many of his fellow Congregationalists, decidedly Jeffersonian. As compiler of two school books, *Patriot's Monitor for Vermont* (1810) and *Patriot's Monitor for New Hampshire* (1810), he spread the Jeffersonian view of American history through those New England states for nearly twenty years. The two *Monitors* reprinted the Declaration of Independence and Washington's address to his army, as well as other speeches of political importance, and liberally interspersed admonitions to filial piety based on the biographies of such founding fathers of northern New England as Vermont's first governor, Thomas Chittenden. Elected to the General Assembly in 1809 as an anti-Federalist, Thomson spoke vigorously against the elitist and exclusivist tendencies in Vermont churches and society.

In the years preceding the War of 1812, the University of Vermont, under the leadership of President Daniel C. Sanders, experienced a variety of difficulties when Sanders rejected certain Congregational ministers' efforts to gain exclusive control of the college for their church and party. The Reverends Asa Burton, Leonard Worcester, and Publius Virgilius Booge objected to Sanders as being, first, a Unitarian, and second, a Harvard man. On both counts, they charged in 1810, Sanders should have been found unsuited for the office of president.

The anti-Sanders forces achieved a dubious victory in 1810. By a narrow margin, the Board of Trustees voted to compel Sanders to attend chapel mornings and evenings. Later in 1810, however, Burton's forces themselves resigned from the Board, thereby leaving the management of the College to the General Assembly. Burton, Booge, and Worcester were immediately chosen trustees of Middlebury College.

DATE: 1813

LOCATION: Vermont Historical Society

SIZE: 27.5 x 22.5 cm.

Dreams, Visions, Providences, Narrative Poems

A DREAM, OR VISION,

By Samuel Ingalls, *of Dunham, in the Province of Lower Canada, on the night of Sept.* 2, 1809.

I Thought I was standing on the bank of White River, in the State of Vermont, about the distance of a mile from the junction of that River with Connecticut River, in company with my brother James Ingalls. I heard a rushing noise in the air; and instantly casting my eyes upward, there appeared to my view three carriages of polished gold, (in the form of the top of a chaise without wheels) passing through the air in a direct line abreast, and steering toward the South. The workmanship of the carriages was exceedingly curious, similar to banister or wicker-work. The distance between each carriage appeared to be about six or eight feet.

In the carriage next to me there were three women elegantly attired; the woman who sat in the centre was considerably larger than either of the other two.

In the middle carriage were three men richly arrayed; the largest was in the centre.

In the third carriage were three Angels, as I supposed by their having wings suspended from their shoulders; the largest Angel was in the centre; their apparel was so shining or glistening as to surpass my power of description. Each Angel held in his hand a wand or sceptre of burnished gold, of curious workmanship, to appearance about six or seven feet in length. Each Angel wore, on his head, a crown or diadem of gold; and on the front of each crown was an erect frontispiece, with large letters or characters written thereon, which I could not understand.

As they passed through the air, I could distinctly hear the Angels sing a hymn, but I can recollect only a part of the tune, and only these words of the hymn: "*Prepare to give me room, ye nations, I am coming!*"

I stedfastly kept my eyes upon them, until I saw them descend in their carriages on the west bank of Connecticut River, in the town of Hartford, in Vermont. I could plainly discern that the Angels were about breast high above the buildings; but the other two carriages, at this time, were lost to my view.—The Angels stretched out their wands or sceptres over Connecticut River, and conversed together a considerable time, but I could hear nothing distinctly, except a tremendous sound. I saw the houses on the east or opposite shore of Connecticut River, in New-Hampshire, totter and shake as if there had been an earthquake, and appeared to me to threaten immediate destruction; but none of the buildings fell to the ground.

They all then arose in their carriages, and I very distinctly heard them pronounce these words—"*This wicked club, who are laying plots to deceive the nations, shall immediately be cut off, and utterly destroyed.*"-While pronouncing these words their carriages stood still; but when the sentence was finished, they arose in their carriages about the height of a tree, and proclaimed these words—"*Thus saith* God, *I will spare the rest of this wicked generation one hundred and forty years, saith the* Lord"—And immediately they all went up out of my sight.

This is really a Dream or Vision which I Samuel Ingalls had, while sleeping, in the night of the 2d of September, 1809.

FERVENTLY Federalists in their opposition to President Thomas Jefferson's hated Embargo through the harsh winters of 1808–09, many New Englanders proposed a convention for nullification of the least successful of Jefferson's diplomatic weapons. Early in 1809 town meetings across Vermont passed resolutions threatening secession. Finally, three days before his term expired on March 4, Jefferson repealed the Embargo Act.

Contrary to its intentions, the Embargo strengthened the pro-British attitudes of New England's Federalists. Republicans supporting Jefferson in Vermont knew well the minority position they held in their communities. After James Madison succeeded Jefferson to the presidency and then failed to negotiate a treaty with England in the summer of 1809, Samuel Ingalls' vision of imperial avenging angels descending the Connecticut River from Canada to support Federalists in their struggle for controlling power appealed to many Vermonters

Federalist newspapers, like the Montpelier *Watchman,* warned of "Democratic [Republican] societies" acting as "instruments of Napoleon." Meanwhile, the Bennington *World*, a Jeffersonian Republican journal sharing Ingalls' vision of a "wicked club, who are laying plots to deceive the nations," called for committees of public safety to deal with "domestic traitors." The effects of these threats from both sides of this dispute, however, were actually no more destructive than the angels in Samuel Ingalls' dream vision: they appeared "to threaten destruction; but none of the buildings fell to the ground."

DATE: 1809

LOCATION: Vermont Historical Society

SIZE: 25.5 X 22.5 cm.

THE GRECIAN DAUGHTER;

Or, an example of a VIRTUOUS WIFF, who fed her Father with her own milk---he being commanded to be ſtarved to death by *Tiberius Cæſar*, Emperor of Rome; but was afterwards pardoned, and the Daughter highly rewarded.

IN Rome there liv'd a Nobleman,
The Emp'ror did offend,
And for that fault he was adjudged
Unto a cruel end.
That he ſhould be in priſon caſt
With irons many a one,
And there be famiſhed unto death,
And brought to ſkin and bone.
And more, if any one were known,
By night, or eke by day,
To bring him any kind of food
His hunger to allay:
The Emperor ſwore a mighty oath,
Without remorſe, quoth he,
*They ſhall ſuſtain the hardeſt death
That can deviſed be.
This cruel ſentence thus pronounced,
This Nobleman was caſt
Into a dungeon, deep and dark,
With irons fettered faſt,
Where when he had with hunger great
Remained ten days ſpace,
And taſted neither meat nor drink,
In a moſt woful caſe.
The tears along his aged face
Moſt piteouſly did fall,
And grievouſly he did begin,
Complaining thus to call:
O Lord, quoth he, what ſhall I do?
So hungry now am I;
For want of bread, one bit of bread,
I periſh, ſtarve and die.
How precious is one grain of wheat,
Unto a hungry ſoul!
One cruſt, or crum, or little piece,
My hunger to controul.

Had I this dungeon heaped with gold,
I now would give it all,
To buy and purchaſe one ſmall loaf,
Yea were it e'er ſo ſmall.
O that I had but every day,
One bit of bread to eat,
Tho' ne'er ſo mouldy, black or brown,
My comfort would be great.
Yes, though obliged to take it up,
Trod down in dirt and mire,
It would be pleaſing to my taſte,
And ſweet to my deſire.
O Lord, moſt happy is the hind,
That labors all the day:
The drudging mule, the peaſant poor,
That at command do ſtay;
They have their ordinary meals,
They take no heed at all
Of thoſe ſmall crumbs&cruſts that they
Do careleſsly let fall.
How happy is the little chick,
Who without fear doth go,
And pick up many precious crumbs
Which they away do throw.
O that ſome pretty little mouſe,
So much my friend would be,
To bring ſome old forſaken cruſts
Into this place to me.
But O my heart, it is in vain,
No ſuccour can I have:
No meat, no drink, nor water eke,
My loathed life to ſave.
O bring ſome bread for Jeſus' ſake,
Some bread, ſome bread to me;
I die, I die for want of food,
None but ſtone walls I ſee.

Thus night and day he conſtant cry'd
In ſuch outrageous ſort;
That all the people far and near
Were grieved at his report.
Though great and many friends he had,
And daughters in the town,
Yet none durſt come to ſuccour him,
Fearing the Emp'ror's frown.
Yet now behold one daughter dear,
He had, as we do find;
Who liv'd in his diſpleaſure great,
Not wedding to his mind:
Altho' ſhe liv'd in me[illegible] eſtate,
She was a virtuo[illegible] wife,
And for to help her Father dear
She ventur'd thu[illegible] life:
She quickly to her ſiſte[illegible] went,
And of them did entreat,
That by ſome ſecret means they would
Convey their Father meat:
Our Father he doth ſtarve, ſaid ſhe,
The Emp'ror's wrath is ſuch,
He dies, alas, for want of food,
Whereof we have too much.
Pray ſiſters therefore uſe ſome means,
His life for to preſerve;
And ſuffer not our Father dear
In priſon for to ſtarve.
Alas, ſaid they, what ſhall we do,
His hunger to ſuſtain.
You know 'tis death for any one,
That would his life maintain,
And tho, we wiſh him well, ſaid they
We never will agree,
To ſpoil ourſelves. we would as ſoon.
That he ſhould die as we;

And ſiſter, if you love yourſelf,
Let this attempt alone:
Tho' you do ne'er ſo ſecret work,
In time it will be known,
O hath our Father brought us up,
And nouriſh'd us, quoth ſhe;
And ſhall we now forſake him quite,
In his extremity!
No, I will venture life and limb,
To do my Father good;
The worſt that is, *I* can but die,
For him *I*'ll ſhed my blood.
With that in haſte away ſhe flies,
And to the priſon goes:
But with her diſmal Father dear,
She might not ſpeak, God knows,
Except the Emperor would grant
Her Father in that caſe,
The keeper would admit no one,
To enter in that place.
Then ſhe unto the emp'ror hies,
And falling on her knees,
With wringing hands and bitter cries
Theſe words pronounced ſhe:
"My helpleſs Father, ſovereign Sir,
Offending of your Grace:
Judg'd to endure a pining death,
Within a diſmal place;
Which *I* confeſs he has deſerv'd,
Yet mighty Prince, ſaid ſhe,
Vouchſafe in gracious ſort to grant,
One ſimple Boon to me:
It chanced ſo *I* match'd myſelf
Againſt my Father's mind,
Whereby *I* did procure his wrath,
As fortune has aſſign'd.

And ſeeing now the time is come
He muſt reſign his breath,
Vouchſafe that *I* may ſpeak to him,
Before the hour of death.
And reconcile myſelf to him,
His favor to obtain,
That when he dies I may not then
Under his curſe remain.
The Emp'ror granted her requeſt,
Conditionally that ſhe
Each day unto her father went,
Should thoroughly ſearched be.
No meat nor drink ſhe with her bro't
To help him there diſtreſt,
But every day ſhe nouriſh'd him
With milk from her own breaſt.
Thus by her milk he was preſ[illegible]'d
A twelve-month and a day:
And was ſo fair and fat to ſee,
Yet none could tell which way.
The Emp'ror muſing much thereat,
At length did underſtand,
How he was fed—and not his laws
Were broke at any hand.
And much admired at the ſame,
And her great virtues ſhown,
He pardon'd him and honor'd her
With great preferments known.
Her father ever after that,
Lov'd her as his own life;
And bleſt the day that ſhe was made
A virtuous loving wife.

PRINTED AT WINDSOR, VERMONT.
1810

NUMBER 19

FROM the passage of the Embargo Act in 1807 until the end of the War of 1812, smuggling contraband goods in and out of Canada was not only a necessary means of marketing Vermont's produce and supplying essential foreign imports but also an obvious expression of dissatisfaction with national policies affecting Vermont. Before the war broke out in 1812, anti-Jeffersonian newspapers expressed tolerance of, sometimes even applauded, smugglers and condemned government enforcement officers as repressors of individual liberties. Even during the war, when contraband trade with Canada was obviously treasonous, Sir George Prevost could inform London from Montreal that the British army in Canada received two thirds of its beef from Vermont. An observer from Burlington, speaking in the pages of the *New Hampshire Sentinel* (May 14, 1808), asked of the embargo, "Why this severe restriction upon our small, but absolutely necessary commerce with Canada?"

The smuggler, then, could be seen by many Vermonters as a noble figure, a hero opposing the restrictive rule of a Jefferson or a Tiberius. Like the "Virtuous Wife, who fed her Father with her own milk," the smuggler brought the necessary trade goods from Canada—the milk—which sustained Vermont until the opening of the Champlain-Hudson Canal expanded opportunities for southern trade with New York markets after the mid-1820's.

Only recently settled but quickly becoming populated, Vermont in 1810 was a combination of frontier egalitarianism and urbane, class-consciousness. Such a mixed audience could easily see the lesson in a broadside drawn from Pliny the Elder's *Naturalis historia.* Conservative Vermonters in need of a cultural tradition to provide a justifying framework of values for their smuggling activities could respond affirmatively to the example from a Latin classic of the virtuous daughter succoring her father. Unread frontiersmen could equally appreciate how resistance to Caesar's repressive rule would bring its own reward.

First printed in 1798 at Windsor, the broadside of the "Virtuous Wife" was one of the most popular documents in the anti-Embargo campaign. It went through three separate printings during the years 1809–10.

DATE: 1810

LOCATION: Vermont Historical Society

SIZE: 49 x 41 cm.

A MONSTER.

FRIGHTFUL AS TEN FURIES!!

TERRIBLE AS HELL!

The following is copied from the JOURNAL kept by Mr. Jacob M. Berriman, during his tour to the Westward of Fort Recovery.

May 27, 1794. THIS morning about an hour after sunrise as we proceeded on our rout about a mile west from the place where we had lodged the preceding night, we were alarmed by a terrible barking of our dogs a-head, & all eagerly pushed forward to take possession of the game thus pionted out by our faithful dogs. About a quarter of a mile a-head we discovered the most terrible Monster which human eyes ever beheld, to which our dogs dare not approach; but only stood barking at a considerable distance. At the sight of so monstrous a creature, every hair on our heads seemed to stand on end with fear: Though we had no reason to apprehend ourselves in danger, for he was busily employed in destroying a large Panter, which seemed as incapable of resistance, as a common squirrel would have been in competition with one our dogs.

We halted, and placed ourselves to the best advantage in order to view his manner of dispatching the Panter, which he did by winding his tail around him and drawing to such a degree as to crush and break his bones, which we could frequently hear sounding like the snapping of a whip, accompanied by the most hidious howls of the agonizing animal. A consultation was next held in order to choose the most effectual method of attacking so formidable an enemy. It was finally determined, that one of the company should go back to the house and procure a horse, on which one of us, being mounted and armed with a musket, should approach within a convenient distance of the snake, and giving him a well-aimed shot, should retreat precipitately in case he was attacked.—Accordingly the person appointed, proceeded back to the house, and in less than an hour returned mounted on a horse well calculated for the purpose. It was then concluded to suspend our attack till he should have devoured his game; which he did in the following manner;—After having broken all his bones, as above, he licked him with his mouth till he appeared all over wet and slippery, and then swallowed him without much difficulty. The large animal which he had now gorged appeared to have greatly abated the agility of his motion, which we thought a circumstance much in our favor;—but on the other hand, we were not without great apprehensions of his scales being so hard that a ball could not penetrate them—However, having mounted the horse myself, I attacked him in the manner above described, and, after giving him three shots, he was so far disabled that we all approached with long gads, and dispatched him without much further difficulty. It was not till about two o'clock in the afternoon, that we accomplished a part of our business so satisfactory, both to our fears and curiosity—. We had now an opportunity to view him leisurely, and such a mixture of horror and beauty, I believe was never before seen blended in one object. After we had drawn him out straight, we proceeded to measure his dimensions, which we did exactly, and found him to be no less than 36 feet 2 inches in length and the largest part of his body to be 3 feet 1 inch in diameter—His eyes were indiscribably large and piercing—His head was of a most beautiful changeable green, towards the top inclining to a yellow, but darker towards his neck and round his jaws—Upon the top of his head was a large oval black spot—His neck was incircled with three rows of spots of the most beautiful crimson—His back, from his neck nearly to the end of his tail was covered with scales of the most beautiful green I ever beheld, on each side was a row of large black scales between two small red stripes. His belly was perfectly white along the middle, but bearing upon a yellow towards each side. The next part of our business was to determine upon the best manner to dispose of the skin, which we looked upon as a most valuable part of our game.

As the day was so far spent that we could not complete the skinning of it before dark, and as we could not possibly carry it away whole, we concluded to leave it until morning. Accordingly we went back to the abovementioned hut, and in the morning returned with knives, and in about three hours we completed the business to our satisfaction. The skin we carefully washed and stuffed it with hay until it was dry, when we opened and rolled it up for the convenience of carrying.

☞ As many perfons, perhaps, will doubt the truth of the above account, they may fatisfy themfelves by calling at Mr. PEAL's Mufeum in Philadelphia, where the Skin was prefented.

PRINTED AND SOLD AT WINDSOR—(VT.)
1812.

NUMBER 20

THE broadside recounting Jacob Berriman's destruction of a monstrous, panther-eating snake "Westward of Fort Recovery" in the spring of 1794 was an instructive message for Vermonters during the opening days of the War of 1812. "The Second War of Independence" threatened Vermont and the nation just as seriously as the events during the last phase of the first War in the 1790's, action of which had taken place on the Maumee at about the same time that Berriman was supposed to have observed the monster frightful as ten furies.

In 1792 General Hugh St. Clair, with the entire United States regular army of 2,000 men, was gravely defeated a few miles from Fort Wayne. After occupying American posts in the Northwest Territory, the British governor of Canada proposed in late 1792 that the land between the Great Lakes and the Ohio River, as well as parts of New York and Vermont, be established as an Indian state. Lieutenant Governor Simcoe of Upper Canada built a fort on the Maumee 100 miles southwest of Detroit. Thus the British imperial monster was prepared to devour a meal that would include the Vermont catamount. In 1812 the feline emblem was familiar to Vermonters and recalled Jonas Fay's tavern, the site of war councils under the sign of the panther in the first War of Independence.

Reorganized after St. Clair's defeat, the United States army under the command of "Mad Anthony" Wayne prepared to battle the imperial monster in the shape of an Indian force with Canadian and British support on the Maumee in the spring of 1794. Mounted riflemen from Kentucky joined Wayne's force, and after a series of encounters throughout the spring and early summer across the Erie plain and Wayne's construction of Fort Defiance, the Americans, with mounted troops leading the attack on the flanks, defeated the British and Indian force at the Battle of Fallen Timbers on August 20, 1794. Finally, after a conference of nearly six weeks in the summer of 1795, nearly twenty years of fighting with England in the first War of Independence came to an end and the fifteen United States acquired from the Indians, for $10,000, portions of the Northwest Territory, Detroit, and the future site of Chicago.

As the war broke out with England in 1812, the parallels with that earlier war were clear in the minds of many Americans. "A Monster . . . Terrible As Hell" threatened again, and Vermonters were to be made aware of it through the emblematic story from Jacob Berriman's *Journal*. Proof of the tale was the stuffed skin on exhibit in Philadelphia at the Museum of Charles Wilson Peale, the famous painter whose portraits of Washington as general and defender of independence would bring courage to the hearts of those who feared the return of the all-devouring serpent.

DATE: 1812

LOCATION: Vermont Historical Society

SIZE: 48.5 x 24.5 cm.

THE HYPOCRITE'S LOOKINGGLASS.

Designed and Engraved by Isaac Eddy

EXPLANATION OF THE PLATE.

The Tything-Man Unmasked;

OR

The Devil's Herald mounted upon Hell's Hobby in the execution of his Infernal Offices,

Armed with a spear stained with the blood of innocence, and representing robbery and extortion.

THE DEVIL IN HIS REAR, STIMULATING HIM TO ACTION, BY RECOMMENDING "HYPOCRICY AND PRIEST-CRAFT."

FURTHER EXPLANATION.

THE Tything-man divested of his superficial robe of righteousness; his frightful and disgusting form exposed in its real* light; his tongue unrestrained by hypocricy disclosing the accursed purposes of his soul, and exclaiming, "When I move, it is in wrath; when I pause, it is amid ruin; my prayers are curses; my God is a demon; my communion is death; my decalogue is written in the blood of my victims; and if I stop for a moment in my infernal flight, it is to whet my virulent fangs for keener rapine, and more sanguinary desolation...Death and devastation are the proceeds of my relentless heart!

"With this spear I raise the cries and augment the distresses of the poor: with this I destroy the effects, and pull down the house of the widow; with this I rob the fatherless and take even from the orphan the last morsel of bread. As the Lion lieth in wait for prey, so do I also to surprise the unwary traveller; as the voracious Tiger gormandises on the victims of his rage; so do I also gorge on the spoils of the stranger, and the way faring man; and as the vulture feasteth on the dead carcase, so do I also filch the remains of the deceased. Yet with blood my burning thirst is unquenched, and with gorging my insatiable appetite is never satisfied.

"My throat is an open sepulchre; with my tongue I have used deceit; the poison of asps is under my lips; my mouth is full of cursing and bitterness: my feet are swift to shed blood, destruction and misery are in my ways: and there is no fear of God before my eyes."

* The design was partially drawn from the description given by St. Paul, of false teachers, in which he says they are dogs, the tail being omitted to preserve the beauty of the plate.

TO THE VOTARIES OF SUPERSTITION AND THE CLERICAL BANDITTI.

Your rapacity has at length become insupportable;—the peaceable traveller, while pursuing his lawful avocation is insulted, way-laid and robbed. Innocence, or even merit, afford him no protection; the claims of justice, and the voice of reason have no effect upon consciences like yours hardened in iniquity, and minds long versed in the practice of wrong and extortion. Remonstrances however reasonably urged, or movingly couched, have had no more influence upon your hearts, than the gentle evening breeze has upon the oak, when it whispers among its branches, or the rising surges upon the deaf rock, when they dash and break against its sides.

You have polluted the communion table of the God whom you profess to worship, and whose decrees you pretend to enforce, and supported the propagators of your ridiculous doctrines, by the unhallowed produce of your hellish robberies; and through your means the temple of Jehovah presents a disgusting scene of unbridled fraud and corruption. No arts are too mean, no persecution too virulent, and no fury too unrelenting to be employed by your infernal banditti in the acquisition of an ascendency over the minds of a deluded multitude. Your whole system of religion portrays but one theme of crimes; nor are the untamed passions of the savage more ferocious, or more vindictive than those of you pretended christians. But the complaints of the unfortunate victims of our intolerance, like the pious orisons of the martyred Abel, ascend to heaven; they cry aloud for vengeance; and think you, that mock devotions and impious vows, can shield from its thunders, you who oppress in the name of the law, and rob in the name of God?

You have endeavored to propogate a belief, that your uncommon energy was stimulated by a desire to support the pure principles of religion and morality; but oppressive indeed, must be that religion and corrupt that morality which is supported by robbery, and which flourishes upon the miseries of mankind....Think not to deceive an enlightened people by *professions* of piety....they are not degenerated to that age of ignorance, superstition and error, when at the fiat of Bigotry, the bonds of friendship were dissolved, and society warred against itself; when fathers became informers against their children, and wives against their husbands, to screen themselves from the menace of destruction; when those who doubted the purity of their doctrines were dragged by the unfeeling arm of clerical power, to have their doubts dispelled by the application of the torture; and forced upon the polluted altars of religion, to utter vows of abjuration blasphemous to the almighty! Think not, that your dark designs will not be unveiled; think not that your damnable hypocricy will escape the prying eye of candor. No. Your villainy must be exposed in all its hideous deformity! Then tremble villains, for hell boasts no miscreants more guilty than yourselves; even Belzebub holds down his head abashed at being outdone by human devils.

CIRCULAR,

TO THE ENLIGHTENED SUPPORTERS OF THE PURE PRINCIPLES OF RELIGION AND MORALITY.

YOU behold a formidable combination of the professed believers of one particular doctrine, formed for the express purposes of annihilating every vestige of power in the civil government, and placing it in their own hands. It is not enough that they are allowed the same privileges which are enjoyed by the professors of other tenets: it is not enough that they are supported by stipulated salaries, but all must bow with submissive deference to *their* superior claims, all must feel the weight of their oppressive arrogance, and the hand that feeds them must perish. Intent on their favorite projects, they are endeavoring to accomplish them by a system of fraud, oppression and persecution unheard of in the annals of intolerance.

Under the sanction of this sect, highwaymen have been organized and let loose upon our unoffending citizens, who have been robbed of the last cent, and every thing of their apparel to gratify the insatiable avarice of these detestable monsters! Even in the boasted "land of steady habits," our brave seamen, after having fought, bled and contributed their share to the laurels which encircle the American navy; after having been, by the fate of war, separated from their country for years; after being landed on their native shores, destitute of the necessary means of subsistence, and while peaceably pursuing their journies to their families and friends, these meritorious supporters of their country's glory, have been seized by the accursed miscreants, in defiance of every principle of hospitality and gratitude, and finding they possessed nothing worth plundering, were doomed to breathe the noxious air of a dungeon, less pestilential than the breath of Bigotry. This is no "fiction wove in fancy's loom"...it is the plain story of their wrongs. Yet with these enormities staring you in the face, and these facts ringing in your ears, with the yoke of oppression still galling your necks and your chains clanking at your heels, can you look calmly on in listless apathy, and survey the triumphs of Superstition, whose look is as petrifying as the fabled head of Medusa, whose touch is the hand of death, and whose march is more desolating than the [illegible] blast of Egypt? No! You must be made familiar with slavery; you must be deaf to the reiterated complaints of [illegible] humanity; you must be degraded to the situation of the brute, and must forget that you are men, before you are ripe for the exhibition of scenes of rapine and plunder, under the pretended sanction of the name of Omnipotence.

Suffer a religious aristocracy to be but once established, and the protecting arm of civil law, will be paralized by the leprous poisons of vice and corruption; and life, liberty and property, the imprescriptible rights of every one, are destined to bleed at the shrine of superstition. You will acquire the stain of accumulated barbarism, and the corrosive reflection of having deserved every misery you endure.

You cannot have the impious folly to believe the almighty so destitute of power, as to require *their* aid in enforcing his laws; or so destitute of regard for mankind as to appoint them

'The chosen few

'To deal Oppression's poison'd arrows round;

'To gall with iron bonds the weaker crew—

'Enforce submission and inflict the wound.'

No longer permit this tyrannical sway of ecclesiastical power. Release from the fell villains' grasp the oppressed travellers who have so long groaned beneath their merciless intolerance; and, as they have existed by rapine, let them die as malefactors; as they have violated religion, they will despair of its consolation; having barbarized nature, they will be execrated by mankind. Bid Superstition's haggard visage disappear, and prevent your country from cherishing so foul a demon within its bosom. Disavow those proceedings, which, while under the officious pretext of enlightening you, only serve to render 'darkness visible'; dissipate the dank mists of bigotry which are fast obscuring the glorious luminary of morality. Let a system of universal benevolence predominate. Cease from entrusting your salvation to the profligacy of interested priests; and under the benign reign of morality, one church arises, to which all flock, all prostrate themselves before one almighty being. With what soothing pleasure, with what enthusiasm! must the philanthropist hail the period when persecution shall be no more! The period when unawed by sanguinary proscription, all descriptions of men, the pagan, the jew, the christian and the turk, shall be securely sheltered within the pale of toleration.

IT is among the votaries of superstition, that we behold the capital villains, the heighth of avarice and extortion, and even the pinacle of human depravity. It is they, that instead of alleviating the distresses of the poor, augment their miseries; that instead of soothing the afflictions of the widow, aggravate her misfortunes; that instead of administering to the necessities of the fatherless, take from them the scanty means of their subsistence; that instead of fostering the orphan, mock his cries! and it is they, that by unrestrained habits of criminality, become callous to every solicitation of humanity; and by the repeated commission of almost every species of cruelty, become obdurate, like the butcher that relenteth not at the lowing of the ox, nor at the bleating of the lamb.

Will you after a long series of admonitions and cautions, by an unguarded stupidity cause you morning sun to go down at noon? Will you

For remainder, see Supplement.

With whatever reception this sheet may meet the public; yet of the "clerical banditti" and their base accomplices, I ask no favors. But of the moral and enlightened part of community, I respectfully solicit their patronage and support.

With philanthropy and respect,
I am the public's most obliging,
most obedient and very
humble servant,
ISAAC EDDY.

NUMBER 21

Isaac Eddy (1777–1847), engraver and publisher of the plate entitled "The Hypocrite's Looking-Glass" (1815), was a Vermonter of primitive but varied talents. In 1814 he bought from Alden Spooner the press on which the famous Dresden Imprints had been produced. Moving the press from Hanover, New Hampshire, to the hamlet of Greenbush in the town of Weathersfield, Eddy began work there as engraver, printer, and experimenter in natural science.

Between 1812 and 1818 Eddy produced engraved illustrations for a curious mixture of publications from, first, the press of Preston Merrifield and James Cochran in Windsor, and then from the Spooner press in Greenbush. In 1812 he illustrated John Russell's *Authentic History of the Vermont State Prison*. Russell was only nineteen years old at the time, and the income from sales of his history helped pay his expenses through Middlebury College. An 1812 edition of the Bible printed by Merrifield and Cochran with Eddy's engravings similarly demonstrate his undeveloped talent.

A venture in radical politics, "The Hypocrite's Looking-Glass" attacks the Congregational establishment in Vermont. Eddy's unorthodox attitude suggests that his illustrations to an 1817–18 Vermont imprint of "Fanny Hill," printed by Jesse Cochran of Windsor, are "Treasures" for Vermont bibliophiles to seek. He is also known to have experimented with that nineteenth-century equivalent of the alchemist's philosopher's stone—the perpetual motion machine.

DATE: 1815

LOCATION: Vermont Historical Society

SIZE: 43 x 62 cm.